Slow cooking

Published by Murdoch Books®, a division of Murdoch Magazines Pty Ltd.

Murdoch Books® Australia
Pier 8/9, 23 Hickson Road
Millers Point NSW 2000
Telephone: + 61 (0) 2 4352 7000
Fax: + 61 (0) 2 4352 7026

Murdoch Books UK Limited
Erico House, 6th Floor North
93/99 Upper Richmond Road
Putney, London, SW15 2TG
Telephone: + 44 (0) 20 8785 5996
Fax: + 44 (0) 20 8785 5995

Art Direction: Marylouise Brammer
Photographer: Alan Benson
Stylist: Mary Harris
Food Preparation: Joanne Glynn
Food Editors: Lulu Grimes, Jane Lawson
Editorial Director: Diana Hill
Editor: Lucy Campbell
Production: Megan Alsop

Recipes developed by Rekha Arnott; Sophie Braimbridge; Joanne Glynn; David Herbert;
Deh-Ta Hsiung; Jane Lawson; Carol Selva Rajah; Priya Wickramasinghe; and the
Murdoch Books Test Kitchen

ISBN 1 74045 441 3

Printed by Sun Fung Offset Binding Company Ltd. PRINTED IN CHINA
Paperback edition first printed 2004
First printed 2003. ©Text, design, photography and illustrations Murdoch Books 2003.

The publisher would like to thank the following for their assistance with this book:
AEG Kitchen Appliances; Breville Holdings Pty Ltd; Chief Australia; Kitchen AID;
Kalinka Gallery; Peppergreen Trading.

IMPORTANT: Those who might be at risk from the effects of salmonella poisoning
(the elderly, pregnant women, young children and those suffering from immune
deficiency diseases) should consult their GP with any concerns about eating raw eggs.

Slow
cooking

Joanne Glynn

Photography Alan Benson

Styling Mary Harris

MURDOCH
B O O K S

Prepare, relax, enjoy 7

Starting well 9

On the stove 29

In the oven 83

Perfect sides 143

A happy ending 165

Glossary and index 187

Prepare, relax, enjoy

Slow cooking is cooking as alchemy. Time, care and the very best ingredients transform a meal and its preparation into purest culinary perfection. It is also cooking as therapy. Begin your slow cooking experience by settling down to pore carefully over this collection of inspiring recipes — classic and modern, savoury and sweet. Once you have made your considered selection, then comes the pleasure of searching for the perfect ingredients. Shopping should not be a supermarket snatch and grab affair. Seek out the suppliers of the best and freshest (and often the simplest) produce. Having carried your prizes home, transform the usually tedious process of preparation into a soothing, satisfying ritual, one that leads you more deeply into the luxurious rhythms of slow cooking. As your food cooks, don't begrudge the time needed for flavours to develop and intensify. This is an opportunity to enjoy some good wine, good company and anticipation of a seriously good meal, so stay close to the kitchen and savour the glorious aromas wafting from the oven or stovetop. And after the anticipation, the finale — luscious, flavourful dishes that reflect the care that went into their creation; food that is a celebration of the art of cooking, and the comfort of home, family and friends.

Starting well

So you've made the decision to slacken the pace and enjoy the kind of slow-cooked meals that have become such a luxury in these hectic, fast-paced times. If it's been a while since you spent time in the kitchen and you're not sure where to begin, try these recipes for starters.

French onion soup

The origins of this soup are uncertain, as several regions of France claim credit for it. Its popularity is indisputable though, as a favourite throughout France — and the rest of the world.

Cooking time 1 hour
Serves 6

50 g (1¾ oz) butter
750 g (1 lb 10 oz) onions, finely sliced
2 garlic cloves, finely chopped
45 g (1½ oz) plain (all-purpose) flour
2 litres (8 cups) beef or chicken stock
1 cup (250 ml) white wine
1 bay leaf
2 sprigs thyme
12 slices day-old baguette
100 g (3½ oz) Gruyère cheese, finely grated

Melt the butter in a heavy-based saucepan and add the onion. Cook over a low heat, stirring occasionally, for 25 minutes, or until the onion is deep golden brown in colour and beginning to caramelize.

Add the garlic and flour and stir continuously for 2 minutes. Slowly blend in the stock and wine, stirring, and bring to the boil. Add the bay leaf and thyme, season, then cover the pan and simmer for 25 minutes. Remove the herbs and check the seasoning. Preheat the grill (broiler).

Toast the baguette slices, then divide among six warmed soup bowls and ladle the soup over the top. Sprinkle with the grated cheese, then put the bowls under the grill until the cheese melts and turns light golden brown.

Minestrone alla Genovese

Just about every region of Italy has its own minestrone. This recipe features a dollop of pesto stirred through at the end; others, such as the Milanese version, use arborio rice instead of pasta.

Cooking time 2½ hours
Serves 6

220 g (8 oz) dried borlotti beans
50 g (1¾ oz) lard or butter
1 large onion, finely chopped
1 garlic clove, finely chopped
15 g (½ oz) parsley, finely chopped
2 sage leaves
100 g (3½ oz) pancetta, cubed
2 celery stalks, halved, then sliced
2 carrots, sliced
3 potatoes, peeled
1 teaspoon tomato paste (purée)
400 g (14 oz) tin chopped tomatoes
8 basil leaves
3 litres (12 cups) chicken or vegetable stock
2 zucchinis (courgettes), sliced
220 g (8 oz) shelled peas
120 g (4½ oz) runner beans, cut into bite-sized lengths
¼ cabbage, shredded
150 g (5½ oz) ditalini or other small pasta
6 tablespoons ready-made pesto
grated Parmesan cheese

Put the dried borlotti beans in a large bowl, cover with cold water and leave to soak overnight. Drain and rinse thoroughly under cold water.

Melt the lard in a large saucepan and add the onion, garlic, parsley, sage and pancetta. Cook over a low heat, stirring once or twice, for about 10 minutes, or until the onion is soft and golden.

Add the celery, carrot and potatoes and cook for 5 minutes. Stir in the tomato paste, tomatoes, basil and borlotti beans. Season with plenty of freshly ground black pepper. Add the stock and bring slowly to the boil. Cover and leave to simmer for 2 hours, stirring once or twice.

If the potatoes haven't already broken up, roughly break them up with a fork against the side of the pan. Taste for seasoning and add the zucchini, peas, runner beans, cabbage and pasta. Simmer until the pasta is al dente. Serve with a dollop of pesto and Parmesan.

Harira (chickpea, lamb and coriander soup)

A light and tasty lunch at any time of the year, a good bowl of soup just can't be beaten. Serve with toasted slices of pitta bread for an authentic taste of the Middle East.

Cooking time 2 hours 25 minutes
Serves 4–6

2 tablespoons olive oil
2 small onions, chopped
2 large garlic cloves, crushed
500 g (1 lb) lamb shoulder steaks, trimmed of excess fat and sinew, cut into small chunks
1½ teaspoons ground cumin
2 teaspoons paprika
½ teaspoon ground cloves
1 bay leaf
2 tablespoons tomato paste (purée)
1 litre (4 cups) beef stock
3 x 300 g (10 oz) tins chickpeas, rinsed and drained
800 g (1 lb 10 oz) tin good-quality chopped tomatoes
30 g (1 oz) finely chopped coriander (cilantro)
coriander (cilantro) leaves
small black olives
toasted pitta bread

Heat the oil in a large, heavy-based saucepan or stockpot, add the onion and garlic and cook for 5 minutes, or until softened. Add the meat, in batches, and cook over a high heat until browned all over. Return all the meat to the pan.

Add the spices and bay leaf to the pan and cook until fragrant. Add the tomato paste and cook for about 2 minutes, stirring constantly. Add the stock to the pan, stir well and bring to the boil.

Add the chickpeas, tomato and chopped coriander to the pan. Stir, then bring to the boil. Reduce the heat and simmer, covered, for 2 hours, or until the meat is tender. Stir occasionally. Season with salt and pepper, to taste.

Garnish with the coriander leaves and small black olives. Serve with toasted pitta bread drizzled with a little extra virgin olive oil.

Previous page: French onion soup, Minestrone alla Genovese
Opposite : Harira (chickpea, lamb and coriander soup)

Beef and beet borsch

Do the Russian thing and serve the borsch with shots of ice-cold vodka.

Cooking time 3½ hours
Serves 8–10

1.25 kg (2 lb 12 oz) beetroot, scrubbed clean
olive oil
1 kg (2 lb 4 oz) beef short ribs
1 large onion, chopped
5 garlic cloves, finely chopped
1¼ teaspoons caraway seeds
2 carrots, finely diced
1 bay leaf
large pinch allspice
1.75 litres (7 cups) beef stock
400 g tin (14 oz) chopped tomatoes
1 tablespoon tomato paste (purée)
1 large potato, diced
3 cups finely shredded red cabbage
¼ cup cider vinegar
½ teaspoon muscavado or other dark brown sugar
¼ cup chopped dill
2 tablespoons finely chopped flatleaf (Italian) parsley
sour cream

Place the beetroot in a large saucepan, cover with water and bring to the boil. Reduce the heat to a steady simmer and cover. Cook for 40 minutes or until tender when pierced with a thin sharp knife. Remove from the heat and allow to cool completely in the cooking liquid.

Meanwhile, brown the ribs in olive oil in a large pot in batches over a high heat, then remove and set aside. Add the onion to the pan and cook until golden. Add the garlic and caraway seeds and cook for another minute, but don't let the garlic burn. Put the beef back in the pan along with any juices, plus the carrots, bay leaf and allspice. Pour over the stock and 1 litre (4 cups) of cold water then bring to the boil. Skim off any scum that floats to the top. Reduce to a simmer and cook, partially covered, for 2–2½ hours or until the meat is very tender. Remove from the heat and carefully lift the beef out of the stock with a slotted spoon. Strain the stock, discarding the vegetables. When cool enough to handle, pull the meat from the bones and set aside. Discard the bones. Remove the beets from their cooking liquid, reserving 1 litre (4 cups) of the liquid. Peel and discard the skins then roughly grate the beets.

Put the stock back on the stove and add the tomatoes, tomato paste, potato, cabbage, grated beets, reserved beet cooking liquid, vinegar and sugar and simmer for 15 minutes or until the potato is tender. Put the beef back in the pan and cook for 10 minutes or until heated through. Stir through the dill and parsley, season and serve with a dollop of sour cream garnished with a little extra dill if desired. Serve with rye or pumpernickel bread.

Prawn bisque

Any seafood lover will appreciate the spectrum of flavours in this bisque, from the sweetness of the brandy to the richness of the prawn butter.

Cooking time 1 hour 10 minutes
Serves 4

120 g (4½ oz) unsalted butter
½ onion, finely diced
½ carrot, finely diced
½ celery stalk, finely diced
1 garlic clove, finely chopped
750 g (1 lb 10 oz) raw prawns (shrimps)
1 tablespoon brandy
1 tablespoon tomato paste (purée)
1 bay leaf
1 tablespoon chopped tarragon
pinch cayenne pepper
200 ml (7 fl oz) dry white wine
75 ml (3½ cups) fish or chicken stock
125 ml (½ cup) thick (double/heavy) cream
pinch cayenne pepper

Heat 25 g (1 oz) of the butter in a saucepan over a high heat until it melts. Add the vegetables and the garlic, cover and cook over a medium-high heat for 5 minutes, or until the vegetables are soft but not coloured. Add the whole prawns and cook for 5 minutes, or until the prawns start to turn pink.

Increase the heat to high, pour in the brandy, allow it to boil, then set it alight with a long match. When the flame is out, add the tomato paste, bay leaf, tarragon and cayenne and stir for 4–5 minutes, or until mixed and the tomato paste changes colour and looks a little dry. Cover with the wine and let it evaporate to a syrup, then add 600 ml (2¼ cups) of the stock. Bring to the boil, reduce the heat, cover and simmer gently for 18–20 minutes. Strain into a bowl, reserving the prawns and liquid separately. Return the liquid to the pan.

Remove the prawns from the strainer and set 10 whole prawns aside to make the prawn butter. Put the remainder in a blender with 125 ml (½ cup) of the reserved liquid. Pulse until blended but still coarse, then strain into the saucepan with the rest of the reserved liquid. Reserve the prawn remnants in the sieve. Return the soup to simmering point while the butter is being made, occasionally skimming any visible oil from the surface with a spoon.

Meanwhile, to make the prawn butter, heat the remaining butter in a small saucepan, add the reserved prawn remnants from the sieve and six of the reserved whole prawns, then sauté for 2–3 minutes, stirring until thoroughly heated. Transfer the mixture to a blender. Purée, then scrape the purée through a fine sieve, mashing with a wooden spoon. Refrigerate the butter mixture until cool and set.

Strain the soup through a fine sieve into a clean saucepan to give it a smooth texture and get rid of the excess oil. Reheat the soup gently, then add the remaining 250 ml (1 cup) of the stock, if desired. Just before serving, whisk in the cream.

Remove the soup from the heat and stir in the prawn butter a teaspoon at a time until it is all mixed in. Season to taste with another pinch of cayenne, and some salt and pepper. Serve immediately with Melba toast, croutons or fresh bread and garnish with a reserved prawn in each bowl.

Bouillabaisse

This famous fish soup is associated with the south of France, particularly Marseille. It is often made with whole fish, such as rascasse (scorpion fish), but it's easier to use fillets.

Cooking time 1 hour
Serves 6

Rouille
1 small red capsicum (pepper)
1 slice white bread, crusts removed
1 red chilli
2 garlic cloves
1 egg yolk
80 ml (⅓ cup) olive oil

Soup
18 mussels
1.5 kg (3 lb 5 oz) firm white fish fillets (red mullet, bass, snapper, monkfish, rascasse, John Dory or eel), skin on
2 tablespoons oil
1 fennel bulb, thinly sliced
1 onion, chopped
750 g (1 lb 10 oz) ripe tomatoes
1.25 litres (5 cups) fish stock or water
pinch saffron threads
bouquet garni
5 cm (2 in) piece of orange zest

To make the rouille, preheat the grill (broiler). Cut the capsicum in half, remove the seeds and membrane and put skin-side-up under the hot grill until the skin blackens and blisters. Leave until cool enough to handle before peeling away the skin. Roughly chop the capsicum.

Soak the bread in 3 tablespoons of water, then squeeze dry with your hands. Put the capsicum, chilli, bread, garlic and egg yolk in a food processor or use a mortar and pestle to pound the mixture together. Gradually add the oil in a thin stream, pounding or mixing until the rouille is smooth and has the texture of thick mayonnaise. Cover and refrigerate.

To make the soup, scrub the mussels and remove their beards. Discard any mussels that are already open and don't close when tapped on the work surface. Cut the fish into bite-sized pieces.

Heat the oil in a large saucepan and cook the fennel and onion over a medium heat for 5 minutes, or until golden.

Score a cross in the top of each tomato. Plunge into boiling water for 20 seconds, then drain and peel the skin away from the cross. Chop the tomatoes, discarding the cores. Add to the pan and cook for 3 minutes. Stir in the stock, saffron, bouquet garni and orange zest, bring to the boil and boil for 10 minutes. Remove the bouquet garni and either push the soup through a sieve or purée in a blender. Return to the cleaned pan, season well and bring back to the boil.

Reduce the heat to a simmer and add the fish and mussels. Cook for 5 minutes or until the fish is tender and the mussels have opened. Throw out any unopened mussels. Serve the soup with rouille and bread.

Risotto nero

You can usually buy the ink sac of squid or cuttlefish from your fish-monger, as well as sachets of ink. Squid ink is a seafood, so don't serve the risotto with Parmesan cheese.

Cooking time 45 minutes
Serves 6

2 medium-sized squid
1 litre (4 cups) fish stock
100 g (3½ oz) butter
1 red onion, finely chopped
2 garlic cloves, crushed
350 g (12 oz) risotto rice
3 sachets of squid or cuttlefish ink, or the ink sac of a large cuttle-fish
150 ml (5 fl oz) white wine
2 teaspoons olive oil

Prepare the squid by pulling the heads and tentacles out of the bodies along with any innards. Cut the heads off below the eyes, leaving just the tentacles. Discard the heads and set the tentacles aside. Rinse the bodies, pulling out the transparent quills. Finely chop the bodies.

Put the stock in a saucepan, bring to the boil and then maintain at a low simmer.

Heat the butter in a large, wide, heavy-based saucepan and cook the onion until softened but not browned. Increase the heat and add the chopped squid. Cook for 3–5 minutes, or until the squid turns opaque. Add the garlic and stir briefly. Add the rice and reduce the heat to low. Season and stir briefly to thoroughly coat the rice.

Squeeze out the ink from the sachets or ink sac and add to the rice with the wine. Increase the heat and stir until all the liquid has been absorbed.

Stir in a ladleful of the simmering stock and cook over a moderate heat, stirring continuously. When the stock has been absorbed, stir in another ladleful. Continue like this for about 20 minutes, until all the stock has been added and the rice is al dente. (You may not need to use all the stock, or you may need a bit extra — every risotto will be slightly different.)

Heat the olive oil in a frying pan and fry the squid tentacles quickly. Garnish the risotto with the tentacles and serve.

Asparagus risotto

This risotto is particularly flavoursome because the asparagus stems are puréed with the stock, which is absorbed by the rice. The addition of cream at the end gives it a rich consistency.

Cooking time 50 minutes
Serves 4

1 kg (2 lb 4 oz) asparagus
500 ml (2 cups) chicken stock
500 ml (2 cups) vegetable stock
4 tablespoons olive oil
1 small onion, finely chopped
350 g (12 oz) risotto rice
75 g (2½ oz) Parmesan cheese, grated
3 tablespoons thick (double/heavy) cream

Wash the asparagus and remove the woody ends (hold each spear at both ends and bend it gently — it will snap at its natural breaking point). Separate the tender spear tips from the stems.

Cook the asparagus stems in boiling water for 8 minutes, or until very tender. Drain and put in a blender with the chicken and vegetable stock. Blend for 1 minute, then put in a saucepan, bring to the boil and maintain at a gentle simmer.

Cook the asparagus tips in boiling water for 1 minute, drain and refresh in iced water.

Heat the olive oil in a large, wide, heavy-based saucepan. Add the onion and cook until softened but not browned. Add the rice and reduce the heat to low. Season and stir briefly to thoroughly coat the rice. Stir in a ladleful of the simmering stock and cook over a moderate heat, stirring continuously. When the stock has been absorbed, stir in another ladleful. Continue like this for about 20 minutes, until all the stock has been added and the rice is al dente. (You may not need to use all the stock, or you may need a little extra — every risotto will be slightly different.)

Add the Parmesan and cream and gently stir in the asparagus tips. Season with salt and pepper and serve hot.

Vegetable terrine with herb sauce

For a terrine that looks as good as it tastes, spend a little time trimming the vegetables to the same size, and arrange the layers neatly and evenly.

Cooking time 40 minutes
Serves 8–10

400 g (14 oz) parsnips, cut into chunks
350 g (12 oz) white sweet potato, cut into chunks
8 large silverbeet (Swiss chard) leaves
6 asparagus spears
3 small zucchinis (courgettes)
8 green beans, topped and tailed
250 g (9 oz) crème fraîche
6 teaspoons powdered gelatine

Herb sauce
1 tablespoon finely chopped parsley
1 tablespoon finely chopped chervil
1 tablespoon finely shredded basil
grated zest of 1 small lemon
300 g (10½ oz) crème fraîche

Cook the parsnip and sweet potato in boiling water for 25 minutes or until tender, then drain and cool. Dip the chard leaves in boiling water, then remove carefully with a slotted spoon and lay flat on tea towels.

Lightly oil a 20 x 7 x 9 cm (8 x 2½ x 3½ in) terrine or loaf tin. Line with a layer of plastic wrap, leaving enough hanging over the sides to cover the top. Then line the tin with the silverbeet leaves, make sure there are no gaps, and leave enough hanging over the sides to cover the top.

Trim the asparagus spears at the thicker ends so they fit the length of the terrine. Slice each zucchini in half lengthways. Steam the asparagus, zucchini and beans for 6 minutes, or until tender to the point of a knife. Drain and refresh in cold water so they keep their colour. Pat dry with paper towels.

Purée the parsnip and sweet potato with the crème fraîche in a food processor, or mash and push through a sieve, and season well. Put 4 tablespoons of water in a small bowl and sprinkle with the gelatine. Leave for 5 minutes until spongy, then put the bowl over a pan of simmering water until melted. Add to the purée and mix well.

Spoon a quarter of the purée into the terrine, then arrange 6 asparagus spears on top, all pointing in the same direction. Smooth over another quarter of purée, then a layer of zucchini, cut sides upwards. Spoon over another layer of purée, then the beans and, finally, the remaining purée. Fold over the overhanging silverbeet leaves and plastic wrap to cover the top. Leave in the fridge overnight. Unmould onto a plate, peel off the plastic wrap and cut into slices.

To make the herb sauce, fold the finely chopped herbs and lemon zest into the crème fraîche and season well. Serve with the vegetable terrine.

Onion tart

Cook the onion slices for the tart slowly to bring out their sweetness, and allow them to turn pale gold in colour.

Cooking time 1 hour 10 minutes
Serves 6

450 g (1 lb) shortcrust pastry
50 g (1¾ oz) butter
550 g (1 lb 4 oz) onions, finely sliced
2 teaspoons thyme leaves
3 eggs
275 ml (9½ fl oz) thick (double/heavy) cream
60 g (2¼ oz) Gruyère cheese, grated
grated nutmeg

Preheat the oven to 180°C (350°F/Gas 4). Line a 23 cm (10 in) fluted loose-based tart tin with the pastry, then line the pastry shell with a crumpled piece of greaseproof paper and baking beads (use dried beans or rice if you don't have beads). Blind bake the pastry for 10 minutes, remove the paper and beads and bake for a further 3–5 minutes, or until the pastry is just cooked but still very pale.

Meanwhile, melt the butter in a small frying pan and cook the onion, stirring, for 10–15 minutes or until tender and lightly browned. Add the thyme leaves and stir well. Leave to cool. Whisk the eggs and cream together and add the cheese. Season with salt, pepper and nutmeg.

Spread the onion into the pastry shell and pour the egg mixture over the top. Bake for 35–40 minutes, or until golden brown. Leave in the tin for 5 minutes before serving.

On the stove

The beauty of these sorts of meals is that, after the initial preparation, you can leave a dish to cook for several hours while you enjoy the company of family and friends.

Stifado

This Greek stew uses a blend of sweet and sour tastes to give it its unique character. Serve the stifado straight from the pot at the table, so that diners can fully savour the exotic aroma as the lid is lifted.

Cooking time 3¼ hours
Serves 6–8

4 tablespoons olive oil
1.8 kg (4 lb) round or chuck beef, in 3 cm (1 in) cubes
1 teaspoon ground cumin
2 onions, finely chopped
3 cloves garlic, crushed
250 ml (1 cup) dry red wine
3 tablespoons tomato paste (purée)
4 tablespoons red wine vinegar
2 cinnamon sticks
10 cloves
2 bay leaves
2 teaspoons sugar
1 kg (2 lb 4 oz) pickling onions
4 tablespoons currants
200 g (7 oz) feta cheese, cut into small cubes

Heat half the oil in a large flameproof casserole dish and brown the beef in batches, adding more oil as needed. Put the beef in a bowl, then sprinkle with the cumin and set aside. Add more oil and soften the onions and garlic over a low heat for 5–6 minutes. Return the meat to the pot.

Stir in the wine, increase the heat and deglaze the pot. Add 500 ml (2 cups) of water, the tomato paste and wine vinegar and bring to the boil. Add the cinnamon, cloves, bay leaves and sugar, and season with salt and freshly ground black pepper. Reduce the heat, cover with a double layer of foil and put the lid on. Simmer over a very low heat for 1 hour.

Peel the onions and cut a cross in the base. Add to the pot along with the currants. Continue cooking for a further 1fi hours, or until the beef is very tender and the sauce is thick. Discard the cinnamon sticks and bay leaves. Stir the cheese in and simmer for 3–4 minutes, uncovered. Taste for seasoning and serve straight from the pot. Serve with rice.

Chilli beef with capsicum, coriander and avocado

A one-pot stew with Central American flavours. The mushrooms enhance its meaty flavour and texture, and the chocolate adds richness. Add extra chilli if you like a little heat.

Cooking time 2 hours
Serves 8

275 g (9¾ oz) red kidney beans
3 tablespoons olive oil
2 onions, chopped
2 fat garlic cloves, crushed
4 medium-hot green chillies, deseeded and finely chopped
110 g (4 oz) dark-gilled field mushrooms, chopped small
800 g (1 lb 12 oz) chuck steak, cubed
2 teaspoons ground cumin
½ teaspoon ground cinnamon
1 teaspoon caster (superfine) sugar
2 bay leaves
2 x 400 g (14 oz) tins chopped tomatoes
200 ml (7 fl oz) beef stock
1 medium-sized red capsicum (pepper), diced
6 tablespoons fresh coriander (cilantro) leaves
25 g (1 oz) dark, bitter chocolate (Mexicanif possible), grated
1 medium firm, ripe avocado
½ red onion, chopped
250 g (9 oz) sour cream

Put the kidney beans in a bowl and cover with cold water. Leave to soak overnight, then drain and rinse. Heat 2 tablespoons of the oil in a large saucepan and add the onion. Cook gently for 10 minutes or until softened and translucent. Add the garlic, chillies and mushrooms and continue to cook for 5 minutes, stirring now and then. Using a slotted spoon, transfer the onion mixture to a plate. Add the remaining oil to the pan and, when very hot, brown the beef in batches.

Return the onion mixture to the pan to join the beef and add the cumin, cinnamon, sugar, bay leaves, tomatoes, stock and beans. Stir together and bring to the boil. Reduce the heat to low, cover and simmer gently for 1 hour. Add the capsicum and simmer for a further 30 minutes.

Stir in 4 tablespoons of coriander and all of the chocolate. Season to taste with salt and extra fresh chilli if desired.

Chop the avocado and mix with the red onion and remaining coriander leaves. Top each serving with a spoonful of sour cream and a spoonful of the avocado mixture.

Tagliatelle with ragù

Spaghetti bolognese is one of the most popular Italian dishes around the world. Interestingly, in Italy the sauce or ragù (which originated in Bologna) is served on tagliatelle.

Cooking time 3½ hours
Serves 4

60 g (2¼ oz) butter
1 onion, finely chopped
1 celery stalk, finely chopped
1 carrot, finely chopped
90 g (3¼ oz) pancetta or bacon, finely chopped
220 g (8 oz) minced (ground) beef
220 g (8 oz) minced (ground) pork
2 sprigs oregano, chopped, or ¼ teaspoon dried oregano
pinch nutmeg
120 g (4 oz) chicken livers, trimmed and finely chopped
125 ml (½ cup) dry white wine
185 ml (¾ cup) milk
400 g (14 oz) tin chopped tomatoes
250 ml (1 cup) beef stock
400 g (14 oz) dried tagliatelle or 500 g (5 lb 2 oz) fresh

Heat the butter in a saucepan and add the onion, celery, carrot and pancetta. Cook over a moderate heat for 6–8 minutes, stirring from time to time.

Add the beef, pork and oregano to the saucepan. Season with salt, pepper and nutmeg. Cook for 5 minutes, or until the meat has changed colour but not browned. Add the chicken livers and cook until it changes colour.

Pour in the wine, increase the heat and boil over a high heat for 2–3 minutes, or until the wine has been absorbed. Stir in 125 ml (½ cup) of the milk, reduce the heat and simmer for 10 minutes. Add the tomatoes and half the stock, partially cover the pan and leave to simmer gently over a very low heat for 3 hours. Add more of the stock as it is needed to keep the sauce moist.

Meanwhile, cook the pasta in a large saucepan of boiling salted water until al dente. Stir the remaining milk into the sauce 5 minutes before serving. Taste the sauce for seasoning, then drain the tagliatelle, toss with the sauce and serve with grated Parmesan cheese.

Boeuf en daube

Daubes are traditionally cooked in squat, earthenware dishes called daubières, but a cast-iron casserole dish with a tight-fitting lid will work just as well.

Cooking time 2¾ hours
Serves 6

Marinade
2 cloves
1 onion, quartered
500 ml (2 cups) red wine
2 strips orange zest
2 garlic cloves
½ celery stalk
2 bay leaves
a few parsley stalks

Daube
1.5 kg (3 lb 5 oz) beef topside, blade or rump
2 tablespoons oil
3 strips pork fat
1 pig's trotter or 225 g (8 oz) piece streaky bacon
700 ml (24 fl oz) beef stock

To make the marinade
Push the cloves into a piece of onion and mix together in a large bowl with the remaining marinade ingredients. Cut the beef into large pieces, season with salt and pepper, add to the marinade and leave overnight.

Heat the oil in a saucepan. Lift the beef out of the marinade and pat dry, then brown in batches in the oil and remove to a plate. You might need to use a little of the marinade liquid to deglaze the pan between batches to prevent bits sticking to the bottom of the pan and burning.

Strain the marinade through a sieve into a bowl and tip the contents of the sieve into the pan to brown. Remove from the pan. Add the marinade liquid to the pan and boil, stirring, for 30 seconds to deglaze the pan.

Put the pork fat in a large casserole dish, then add the pig's trotter, beef and marinade ingredients. Pour in the marinade liquid and stock. Bring to the boil, then cover, reduce the heat and simmer gently for 2–2½ hours or until the meat is tender.

Lift the meat out of the casserole and transfer to a serving dish, cover and keep warm. Discard the garlic, onion, pork fat and pig's trotter. Pour the liquid through a fine sieve and skim off as much fat as possible, then return it to the casserole dish. Bring to the boil and boil until syrupy and reduced by half. Pour the gravy over the meat to serve.

Red-cooked pork

Red-cooking, or braising in a soy-based liquid, is a technique used all over China to make chicken or other meat super tender.

Cooking time 3 hours
Serves 8

1.5 kg (3 lb 5 oz) pork leg, with bone in and rind on
4 spring onions (scallions), each tied in a knot
4 slices fresh ginger, smashed with the flat side of a cleaver
200 ml (7 fl oz) dark soy sauce
4 tablespoons Shaoxing rice wine
1 teaspoon five-spice powder
50 g (1¾ oz) rock sugar

Scrape the pork rind to make sure it is free of any bristles. Blanch the pork in a pan of boiling water for 4–5 minutes. Rinse the pork and put in a clay pot or casserole dish with 600 ml (21 fl oz) of water, the spring onions, ginger, soy sauce, rice wine, five-spice powder and sugar. Bring to the boil, then reduce the heat and simmer, covered, for 2½–3 hours, turning several times, until the meat is very tender and falling from the bone.

If there is too much liquid, remove the pork and reduce the sauce by boiling it for 10–15 minutes. Slice the pork and serve with the sauce poured over it.

Pork noisettes with prunes

This is a typical dish of the orchard-rich Touraine region in France. The sweet prunes combine beautifully with the pork.

Cooking time 40 minutes
Serves 4

8 pork noisettes or 2 x 400 g (14 oz) pork fillets
16 prunes, pitted
1 tablespoon oil
45 g (1½ oz) butter
1 onion, finely chopped
155 ml (5 fl oz) white wine
280 ml (10 fl oz) chicken or brown stock
1 bay leaf
2 sprigs thyme
250 ml (1 cup) thick (double/heavy) cream

Trim any excess fat from the pork, making sure you get rid of any membrane that will cause the pork to shrink. If you are using pork fillet, cut each fillet into four diagonal slices. Put the prunes in a small saucepan, cover with cold water and bring to the boil. Reduce the heat and simmer the prunes for 5 minutes. Drain well.

Heat the oil in a large, heavy-based frying pan and add half the butter. When the butter starts foaming, add the pork, in batches if necessary, and sauté on both sides until cooked. Transfer the pork to a warm plate, cover and keep warm.

Pour off the excess fat from the pan. Melt the remaining butter, add the onion and cook over a low heat until softened but not browned. Add the wine, bring to the boil and simmer for 2 minutes. Add the stock, bay leaf and thyme and bring to the boil. Reduce the heat and simmer for 10 minutes or until reduced by half. Strain the stock into a bowl and rinse the frying pan. Return the stock to the pan, add the cream and prunes and simmer for 8 minutes, or until the sauce thickens slightly. Tip the pork back into the pan and simmer until heated through.

Italian-style spicy sausage and bean casserole

A staple across Italy, no matter what beans are favoured or which sausage is locally preferred, the end result is always hearty and wholesome.

Cooking time 4¾ hours
Serves 6

300 g (10½ oz) dried cannellini beans
300 g (10½ oz) dried black-eyed beans
1 tablespoon olive oil
6 large country pork sausages
6 rashers rindless streaky bacon, cut into 6–7 cm (2–3 in) lengths
4 small onions, quartered from top to bottom
10 whole garlic cloves, peeled
3 long thin carrots, cut into 3 cm (1 in) sections
3 bay leaves
7 sprigs oregano, leaves only
1 small red chilli, split and deseeded
500 ml (2 cups) chicken stock
2 tablespoons tomato paste (purée)

Cover the beans with plenty of cold water and soak overnight. Drain and rinse under cold water. Put in a large stockpot or flameproof casserole dish and cover with cold water. Bring to the boil and simmer for 30 minutes. Drain and reserve until needed.

Heat the oil in the pot and lightly brown the sausages for 4–5 minutes. Remove and reserve. Take the pot off the heat and layer the bacon over the base. Add the onions, garlic and carrots and season well with freshly ground black pepper. Put the sausages on top. Add the bay leaves, half the oregano and chilli. Cover with the beans.

Mix the chicken stock and tomato paste together and pour over the beans. (The contents of the pot won't be covered with liquid at this stage.) Season with salt and pepper, cover and simmer over a low heat for 4 hours. If the liquid level remains below the beans after 1 hour, top it up with hot water to just cover. Give the pot a gentle stir every 45 minutes or so.

Stir and taste for seasoning. Sprinkle the remaining oregano into the pot just before serving.

Previous page: Red-cooked pork, Pork noisettes with prunes
Opposite: Italian-style spicy sausage and bean casserole

Rogan josh

Nothing compares with the aroma and flavour of freshly ground spices. The name of the dish comes from the colour of the chilli powder and paprika, 'rogan' meaning red.

Cooking time 1¼ hours
Serves 6

8 garlic cloves, crushed
6 cm (2 in) piece fresh ginger, grated
2 teaspoons ground cumin
1 teaspoon Kashmiri chilli powder
2 teaspoons paprika
2 teaspoons ground coriander
1 kg (2 lb 4 oz) boneless leg or shoulder of lamb, cut into 3 cm (1 in) cubes
5 tablespoons ghee or oil
1 onion, finely chopped
6 cardamom pods
4 cloves
2 Indian bay leaves (cassia leaves)
8 cm (3 in) cinnamon stick
200 ml (7 fl oz) plain or Greek-style yoghurt
4 strands saffron, mixed with 2 tablespoons milk
¼ teaspoon garam masala

Mix the garlic, ginger, cumin, chilli powder, paprika and coriander in a large bowl. Add the meat and stir thoroughly to coat the meat cubes well. Cover and marinate for at least 2 hours, or overnight, in the fridge.

Heat the ghee or oil in a casserole dish over a low heat. Add the onion and cook for about 10 minutes, or until the onion is lightly browned. Remove from the pan.

Add the cardamom pods, cloves, bay leaves and cinnamon to the pan and fry for 1 minute. Increase the heat to high, add the meat and onion, then mix well and fry for 2 minutes. Stir well, then reduce the heat to low, cover and cook for 15 minutes. Uncover and fry for another 3 minutes, or until the meat is quite dry. Add 100 ml (3¼ fl oz) of water, cover and cook for 5–7 minutes, until the water has evaporated and the oil separates out and floats on the surface. Fry the meat for another 1–2 minutes, then add 250 ml (1 cup) of water. Cover and cook for 40–50 minutes, gently simmering until the meat is tender. The liquid will reduce quite a bit.

Stir in the yoghurt when the meat is almost tender, taking care not to allow the meat to catch on the base of the pan. Add the saffron and milk. Stir the mixture a few times to mix in the saffron. Season with salt, to taste. Remove from the heat and sprinkle with garam masala.

Lamb braised with beans

Serve the lamb with a generous helping of potatoes for the most truly satisfying of meals.

Cooking time 3¼ hours
Serves 4

125 g (4½ oz) dried haricot beans
1 x 1 kg (2 lb 4 oz) boned shoulder of lamb, tied with string to keep its shape
30 g (1 oz) butter
2 carrots, diced
2 large onions, chopped
4 garlic cloves, unpeeled
bouquet garni
250 ml (1 cup) dry red wine
250 ml (1 cup) lamb or beef stock

Put the beans in a large bowl and cover with plenty of water. Leave to soak for 8–12 hours, then drain. Bring a large saucepan of water to the boil, add the beans and return to the boil. Reduce the heat to moderate and cook the beans, partially covered, for 40 minutes. Drain well.

Rub the lamb all over with salt and pepper. Heat the butter over a high heat in a large casserole dish with a tight-fitting lid. Add the lamb and cook for 8–10 minutes, turning every few minutes until well browned. Remove the lamb.

Reheat the casserole dish over a high heat and add the carrot, onion, garlic and bouquet garni. Reduce the heat and cook, stirring, for 8–10 minutes or until softened. Increase the heat to high and pour in the wine. Boil, stirring, for about 30 seconds to deglaze the casserole, then return the lamb to the casserole. Add the stock.

Bring to the boil, then cover and reduce the heat to low. Braise for 1½ hours, turning twice. If the lid is not tight fitting, cover the casserole with foil and then put the lid on top.

Add the cooked beans to the lamb and return to the boil over a high heat. Reduce the heat to low, cover the casserole again and cook for a further 30 minutes.

Lift the lamb out of the casserole, cover and leave to rest for 10 minutes before carving. Discard the bouquet garni. Skim the excess fat from the surface of the sauce and, if the sauce is too thin, boil over a high heat for 5 minutes or until thickened slightly. Season to taste. Carve the lamb and arrange on a platter. Spoon the beans around the lamb and drizzle with the gravy. Serve the rest of the gravy separately.

Lamb tagine

In Morocco, a tagine refers both to the stew itself and the earthenware dish in which the stew is simmered. The meat, fish or vegetable stews combine sweet and savoury flavours.

Cooking time 3 hours
Serves 8

50 g (1¾ oz) slivered almonds
4 tablespoons olive oil
2 kg (4 lb 8 oz) boneless lamb shoulder, trimmed and cubed
2 onions, chopped
3 garlic cloves, thinly sliced
3 tablespoons chopped coriander (cilantro)
2 teaspoons ground coriander
2 teaspoons ground cumin
2 teaspoons ground cinnamon
1 teaspoon turmeric
½ teaspoon ground ginger
½ teaspoon cayenne pepper
2 tablespoons ground almonds
1 orange
500 ml (2 cups) chicken stock
180 g (6 oz) pitted dates
4 sprigs coriander (cilantro), torn into leaves
couscous

Heat a large stockpot or flameproof casserole dish and dry-fry the almonds until golden. Reserve. Add half the oil and brown the lamb in batches over a high heat. Season each batch lightly with salt and pepper and transfer to a bowl after each is done.

Heat the remaining oil in the pan and add the onion and garlic. Lower the heat and cook for about 6–8 minutes, until softened. Stir in the chopped and ground coriander, cumin, cinnamon, turmeric, ginger and cayenne and cook for 5 minutes. Return the lamb to the pan and stir the ground almonds through. Grate the zest from the orange and squeeze out the juice. Add both to the lamb and stir the stock in.

Bring to the boil then lower the heat. Cover and simmer gently for 2 hours. Add half the dates and simmer for a further 20 minutes, leaving the lid off if the sauce needs to thicken. The dates will turn to pulp.

Preheat the grill (broiler) to hot and toast the remaining dates for about 3–4 minutes until crusty all over. Stir the toasted almonds into the tagine and scatter the grilled dates and the coriander leaves over the top. Serve with couscous.

Moghul-style lamb

Marinate the lamb, preferably overnight, to ensure that it is tender and full of flavour. Cream is used to temper the strong combination of spices.

Cooking time 1 hour 20 minutes
Serves 4

6 garlic cloves, roughly chopped
4 cm (1½ in) piece fresh ginger, roughly chopped
50 g (1¾ oz) blanched almonds
2 onions, thinly sliced
850 g (1 lb 14 oz) boneless leg or shoulder of lamb, cut into cubes
2 teaspoons coriander seeds
40 g (1½ oz) ghee
7 cardamom pods
5 cloves
1 cinnamon stick
1 teaspoon salt
300 ml (10½ fl oz) cream
½ teaspoon cayenne pepper
½ teaspoon garam masala
flaked almonds, toasted

Blend the garlic, ginger, almonds and 50 g (1¾ oz) of the onion in a blender or food processor. If you don't have a blender, finely chop them with a knife or grind together with a mortar and pestle. Add a little water, if necessary, to make a smooth paste, then put in a bowl with the lamb and mix thoroughly to coat the meat. Cover and marinate in the fridge for 2 hours, or overnight.

Put a small frying pan over a low heat and dry-roast the coriander seeds until aromatic, then grind to a fine powder using a spice grinder or mortar and pestle.

Heat the ghee in a casserole dish. Add the cardamom pods, cloves and cinnamon stick, and, after a few seconds, add the remaining onion and fry until it is soft and starting to brown. Transfer the onion to a plate.

Fry the meat and marinade in the pan until the mixture is quite dry and has started to brown a little. Add 150 ml (5 fl oz) of hot water to the pan, cover tightly and cook over a low heat for 30 minutes, stirring occasionally.

Add the ground coriander, salt, cream, cayenne pepper and cooked onion to the pan, cover and simmer for another 30 minutes, or until the lamb is tender. Stir occasionally to prevent the lamb from sticking to the pan. Remove the cardamom pods, cloves and cinnamon stick, then stir in the garam masala. Sprinkle with flaked almonds before serving.

Osso buco

Osso buco is from northern Italy, a region that does not traditionally use tomatoes in cooking. The absence of tomato allows the more delicate flavour of the gremolata to come through.

Cooking time 1 hour 40 minutes
Serves 4

12 pieces veal shank, about 4 cm (2 in) thick
plain (all-purpose) flour, seasoned, for dusting
60 ml (¼ cup) olive oil
60 g (2¼ oz) butter
1 garlic clove, whole
250 ml (1 cup) dry white wine
1 bay leaf or lemon leaf
pinch allspice
pinch ground cinnamon
thin lemon wedges

Gremolata
2 teaspoons grated lemon zest
6 tablespoons finely chopped parsley
1 garlic clove, finely chopped

Use kitchen string to tie each piece of veal shank around its girth to secure the flesh, then dust with the seasoned flour. Heat the oil, butter and garlic in a large, heavy saucepan big enough to hold the shanks in a single layer. Put the shanks in the pan and cook for 12–15 minutes until well browned. Arrange the shanks, standing them up in a single layer, pour in the wine and add the bay leaf, allspice and cinnamon. Cover.

Cook at a low simmer for 15 minutes, then add 125 ml (½ cup) of warm water. Continue cooking, covered, for about 45 minutes to 1 hour (the timing will depend on the age of the veal), until the meat is tender and you can cut it with a fork. Check the volume of liquid once or twice and add more warm water as needed. Transfer the veal to a plate and keep warm. Discard the garlic clove and bay leaf.

To make the gremolata, mix together the lemon zest, parsley and garlic.

Increase the heat under the saucepan and stir for 1–2 minutes until the sauce is thick, scraping up any bits off the bottom as you stir. Stir in the gremolata. Season to taste and return the veal to the sauce. Heat through, then serve with lemon wedges and Milanese risotto, on page 148.

Sweet paprika veal goulash

Originally from Hungary, a good goulash is tender and creamy with a little bit of bite from the paprika.

Cooking time 3 hours
Serves 6

1.5 kg (3 lb 5 oz) veal shoulder
2 tablespoons butter
2 tablespoons oil
2 large brown onions, chopped
4 garlic cloves, crushed
1½ tablespoons sweet paprika
1 teaspoon caraway seeds
1 bay leaf
2 red capsicums (peppers), seeded and thinly sliced
400 g (14 oz) tin chopped tomatoes
1 tablespoon tomato paste (purée)
310 ml (1¼ cups) beef stock
250 ml (1 cup) red wine
1½ tablespoons red wine vinegar
1 large potato, peeled and diced
sour cream
buttered noodles

Trim the veal of fat and sinew and cut into small cubes. Melt half the butter with the oil in a large, heavy–based saucepan and brown off the veal in batches over a medium–high heat, then set aside. Add the onions to the pan with a little more butter and oil, if needed, and cook over a medium heat, stirring regularly for 10 minutes or until golden.

Add the garlic, paprika, caraway and bay leaf and cook for 1 minute or until the spices are aromatic. Add the meat to the pan with the capsicum, tomato, tomato paste, stock, wine and vinegar and stir to scrape up any pan bits. Bring to the boil and spoon off any scum that floats to the surface. Reduce the heat to low and simmer gently, covered, for 1 hour, lifting the lid to stir occasionally, then cook, uncovered, for a further 1½ hours, stirring occasionally.

Add the potato to the pan in the last half hour. The meat should be very tender but not falling apart. Season and serve with a dollop of sour cream and buttered noodles.

Rabbit fricassée

A fricassée is a dish of white meat, usually chicken, veal or rabbit, in a velouté sauce made with egg yolks and cream. Wild rabbit has a better flavour than farmed.

Cooking time 1 hour
Serves 4

60 g (2¼ oz) clarified butter
1 x 1.5 kg (3 lb 5 oz) rabbit, cut into 8 pieces
200 g (7 oz) button mushrooms
125 ml (½ cup) white wine
125 ml (½ cup) chicken stock
bouquet garni
80 ml (⅓ cup) oil
small bunch of sage
150 ml (5 fl oz) thick (double/heavy) cream
2 egg yolks

Heat half the butter in a large saucepan, season the rabbit and brown in batches, turning once. Remove from the saucepan and set aside. Add the remaining butter to the saucepan and brown the mushrooms.

Put the rabbit back into the saucepan with the mushrooms. Add the wine and boil for a couple of minutes before adding the stock and bouquet garni. Cover the pan tightly and simmer gently over a very low heat for 40 minutes.

Meanwhile, heat the oil in a small saucepan. Remove the leaves from the bunch of sage and drop them, a few at a time, into the hot oil. The leaves will immediately start to bubble around the edges. Cook them for 30 seconds, or until bright green and crispy. Make sure you don't overheat the oil or cook the leaves for too long or they will turn black and taste burnt. Drain the leaves on paper towels and sprinkle with salt.

Lift the cooked rabbit and mushrooms out of the saucepan and keep warm. Discard the bouquet garni. Remove the pan from the heat, mix together the cream and egg yolks and stir quickly into the stock. Return to a very low heat and cook, stirring, for about 5 minutes to thicken slightly (don't let the sauce boil or the eggs will scramble). Season to taste with salt and pepper.

To serve, pour the sauce over the rabbit and mushrooms and garnish with crispy sage leaves.

Coq au vin

It is said that the ancient Romans created this dish to demonstrate their superior sophistication to the Gauls, whose French descendants have since claimed it as their own.

Cooking time 1 hour 25 minutes
Serves 8

2 x 1.6 kg (3 lb 8 oz) chickens
750 ml (1 bottle) red wine
2 bay leaves
2 sprigs thyme
250 g (9 oz) bacon, diced
60 g (2¼ oz) butter
20 pickling or pearl onions
250 g (9 oz) button mushrooms
1 teaspoon oil
30 g (1 oz) plain (all-purpose) flour
1 litre (4 cups) chicken stock
125 ml (½ cup) brandy
2 teaspoons tomato paste (purée)
1½ tablespoons softened butter
1 tablespoon plain (all-purpose) flour

Joint each chicken into eight pieces by removing both legs and cutting between the joint of the drumstick and the thigh. Cut down either side of the backbone and lift it out. Turn the chicken over and cut through the cartilage down the centre of the breastbone. Cut each breast in half, leaving the wing attached to the top half.

Put the wine, bay leaves, thyme and some salt and pepper in a bowl and add the chicken. Cover and leave to marinate, preferably overnight.

Blanch the bacon in boiling water, then drain, pat dry and sauté in a frying pan until golden. Lift out onto a plate. Melt a quarter of the butter in the pan, add the onions and sauté until browned. Lift out and set aside.

Melt another quarter of the butter, add the mushrooms, season with salt and pepper and sauté for 5 minutes. Remove and set aside.

Drain the chicken, reserving the marinade, and pat the meat dry. Season. Add the remaining butter and the oil to the pan, add the chicken and sauté until golden. Stir in the flour.

Transfer the chicken to a large saucepan or casserole dish and add the stock. Pour the brandy into the frying pan and boil, stirring, for 30 seconds to deglaze the pan. Pour over the chicken. Add the marinade, onions, mushrooms, bacon and tomato paste. Cook over a moderate heat for 45 minutes, or until the chicken is cooked through.

If the sauce needs thickening, lift out the chicken and vegetables and bring the sauce to the boil. Mix together the butter and flour and whisk into the sauce. Boil, stirring, for 2 minutes until thickened, then return the chicken and vegetables to the sauce.

Moroccan chicken stew

An aromatic and spicy stew that should be served in bowls with plenty of couscous to soak up the delicious juices. This is truly restorative food.

Cooking time 1½ hours
Serves 4

2 generous pinches saffron threads
875 ml (3½ cups) chicken stock
1.5 kg (3 lb 5 oz) free-range chicken, jointed into 8
2–3 tablespoons olive oil
1 teaspoon coriander (cilantro) seeds
1 teaspoon cumin seeds
2 onions, chopped
4 garlic cloves, peeled and finely chopped
½ teaspoon ground ginger
1 tablespoon soft dark brown sugar
¾ teaspoon harissa
200 ml (7 fl oz) dry white wine
1 cinnamon stick
400 g (14 oz) peeled, cubed butternut pumpkin (squash)
75 g (2½ oz) pitted green olives
1 tablespoon finely chopped preserved lemon
1 tablespoon finely chopped coriander (cilantro)
1 tablespoon finely chopped mint leaves

Put the saffron in a cup and add 2 tablespoons of the stock. Stir and leave to soak. Season the chicken pieces and heat 2 tablespoons of the oil in a large flameproof casserole dish. Brown the chicken in batches until golden, adding another tablespoon of oil if necessary. Set the browned chicken pieces aside on a plate.

Meanwhile, put the coriander seeds in a small frying pan and toast over a medium heat. The spices will start to jump around and smell aromatic when they are ready. Tip into a mortar and pestle or a spice grinder. Dry-roast the cumin seeds, add to the mortar or grinder, then grind both spices to a powder.

Discard all but 1 teaspoon of the oil from the casserole. Add the onion and cook for 5 minutes, stirring now and then. Add the garlic, ginger, sugar, cumin and coriander and cook for a further 2 minutes. Stir in the saffron and its soaking liquid, the harissa, the rest of the chicken stock and the wine. Return the chicken pieces to the liquid, add the cinnamon stick and bring the mixture to the boil. Reduce the heat to a gentle simmer and cover. Leave to simmer gently for 20 minutes.

Add the pumpkin to the liquid and bring back to the boil. Reduce the heat to low and cover. Continue to gently simmer for a further 30 minutes, turning the chicken halfway. When the chicken is ready, the juices of the thigh will run clear when pierced with the point of a small, sharp knife and the pumpkin will be tender.

Using a slotted spoon, transfer the chicken, onion and cinnamon stick to a deep serving dish and keep warm. Put the casserole over direct heat and boil the liquid until it has reduced by approximately two-thirds.

Stir in the olives and preserved lemon and heat gently for a few minutes. Season to taste, adding a little more harissa if desired, and stir in the herbs. Pour the sauce over the chicken and serve.

Cardamom chicken

This dish has a highly aromatic sauce flavoured with cardamom and made deliciously creamy with the addition of yoghurt.

Cooking time 45 minutes
Serves 4

1.5 kg (3 lb 5 oz) chicken or chicken pieces
25 cardamom pods
4 garlic cloves, crushed
3 cm (1 in) piece fresh ginger, grated
300 ml (10½ fl oz) plain or Greek-style yoghurt
1½ teaspoons ground black pepper
grated zest of 1 lemon
2 tablespoons ghee or oil
400 ml (14 fl oz) coconut milk
6 green chillies, pricked all over
2 tablespoons chopped coriander (cilantro) leaves
3 tablespoons lemon juice

If using a whole chicken, cut it into eight pieces by removing both legs and cutting between the joint of the drumstick and thigh. Cut down either side of the backbone and remove the backbone. Turn the chicken over and cut through the cartilage down the centre of the breastbone. Cut each breast in half, leaving the wing attached to the top half. Trim off the wing tips. Remove the skin if you prefer.

Remove the seeds from the cardamom pods and crush them in a spice grinder or with a mortar and pestle. In a blender, mix the garlic and ginger with enough yoghurt — about 125 ml (½ cup) — to make a paste, or mix them with a spoon. Add the cardamom, pepper and grated zest. Spread this over the chicken pieces, cover, and refrigerate overnight.

Heat the ghee or oil in a heavy-based frying pan over a low heat and brown the chicken pieces all over. Add the remaining yoghurt and coconut milk to the pan, bring to the boil, then add the whole chillies and coriander leaves. Simmer for 20–30 minutes or until the chicken is cooked through. Remove from the heat. Season with salt, to taste, and stir in the lemon juice just before serving.

Poulet au pot

This chicken is cooked very simply, so use a free-range bird as you will be able to taste the difference.

Cooking time 1 hour 20 minutes
Serves 4

1 large 1.8–2 kg (4 lb–4 lb 8 oz) free-range chicken
3 litres (12 cups) chicken stock
1 onion, quartered
4 cloves
2 celery stalks, chopped
2 bay leaves
1 kg (2 lb 4 oz) small chat potatoes
3 leeks, cut into 5 cm (2 in) lengths
12 baby carrots
1 tablespoon roughly chopped flat-leaf (Italian) parsley
2 teaspoons thyme leaves
1 teaspoon finely chopped lemon zest

Put the chicken and stock in a large saucepan. Stick each of the onion quarters with a clove and add to the saucepan along with the celery and bay leaves. Bring to the boil, skim and simmer gently for 1 hour.

Remove the chicken to a warm spot and strain the stock. Return the stock to the saucepan and bring to the boil. Add the potatoes and carrots and cook for 10 minutes. Add the leeks and cook for a further 10 minutes or until all the vegetables are cooked. Meanwhile, cut the chicken into serving pieces and keep warm.

To serve, remove the cooked vegetables and put on a large serving dish. Put the chicken pieces on top and pour over the hot stock. Top with the parsley, thyme and lemon zest. Accompany with Dijon mustard and aïoli.

Soy chicken

Marinated in rice wine, soy sauce and sugar, the skin of the chicken turns a rich, dark brown during cooking.

Cooking time 50 minutes
Serves 4

1.5 kg (3 lb 5 oz) chicken
1 tablespoon ground Sichuan peppercorns
2 tablespoons grated fresh ginger
2 tablespoons sugar
3 tablespoons Shaoxing rice wine
310 ml (1¼ cups) dark soy sauce
185 ml (¾ cup) light soy sauce
600 ml (21 fl oz) oil
450 ml (16 fl oz) chicken stock
2 teaspoons roasted sesame oil

Rinse the chicken, drain, and remove any fat from the cavity opening and around the neck. Cut off and discard the parson's nose (the fatty end of the tail). Rub the peppercorns and ginger all over the inside and outside of the chicken. Combine the sugar, rice wine and soy sauces and add the chicken. Marinate in the fridge for at least 3 hours, turning occasionally.

Heat a wok over a high heat, add the oil and heat until very hot. Drain the chicken, reserving the marinade, and fry for 8 minutes until browned. Put in a clay pot or casserole with the marinade and stock.

Bring to the boil, then simmer, covered, for 35–40 minutes. Leave off the heat for 2–3 hours, transferring to the fridge once cool. Drain the chicken, brush with sesame oil and refrigerate for 1 hour.

Using a cleaver, chop the chicken through the bones into bite–sized pieces. Serve with a couple of tablespoons of sauce spooned over the top.

Poulet Vallée d'Auge

A classic dish from Normandy and Brittany — the apple-growing regions of France — which is enriched with Calvados and crème fraîche.

Cooking time 45 minutes
Serves 4

1 x 1.6 kg (3 lb 8 oz) chicken
2 dessert apples
1 tablespoon lemon juice
60 g (2¼ oz) butter
½ onion, finely chopped
½ celery stalk, finely chopped
10 g (¼ oz) plain (all-purpose) flour
80 ml (⅓ cup) Calvados or brandy
375 ml (13 fl oz) chicken stock
100 ml (3½ fl oz) crème fraîche

Joint the chicken into 8 pieces by removing both legs and cutting between the joint of the drumstick and the thigh. Cut down either side of the backbone and lift it out. Turn the chicken over and cut through the cartilage down the centre of the breastbone. Cut each breast in half, leaving the wing attached to the top half.

Peel and core the apples. Finely chop half of one apple and cut the rest into 12 equal wedges. Toss the apple in the lemon juice.

Heat half the butter in a large frying pan, then add the chicken pieces, skin-side-down, and cook until golden. Turn over and cook for another 5 minutes. Lift the chicken out of the pan and tip away the fat.

Heat a slightly smaller slab of butter in the same pan, add the onion, celery and chopped apple and fry over a moderate heat for 5 minutes without browning.

Remove from the heat. Sprinkle the flour over the vegetables and stir in. Add the Calvados and return to the heat. Gradually stir in the chicken stock. Bring to the boil, return the chicken to the pan, cover and simmer gently for 15 minutes, or until the chicken is tender and cooked through.

Meanwhile, heat the remaining butter in a small frying pan. Add the apple wedges and fry over a moderate heat until browned and tender. Remove from the pan and keep warm.

Remove the chicken from the pan and keep warm. Skim the excess fat from the cooking liquid. Add the crème fraîche, bring to the boil and boil for 4 minutes, or until the sauce is thick enough to lightly coat the back of a wooden spoon. Season and pour over the chicken. Serve with the apple wedges.

Previous page: Poulet au pot, Soy chicken
Opposite: Poulet Vallée d'Auge

Duck confit

A confit is the traditional way of preserving meat in its own fat, to be
used throughout the year. Goose meat can also be treated in this way.

Cooking time 2½–3 hours
Serves 6

3 juniper berries, crushed
2 bay leaves, crushed
2 garlic cloves, crushed
2 tablespoons chopped rosemary
3 tablespoons thyme
¼ teaspoon powdered mace or ground nutmeg
12 duck legs or Marylands (leg quarters)
2 kg (4 lb 8 oz) duck or goose fat
4 garlic cloves, crushed
2 tablespoons thyme
lentils
fried apple slices

Mix together the herbs and spices along with a tablespoon each of
salt and freshly ground black pepper. Liberally sprinkle both sides of
the duck legs with the spice mixture and put into a glass, ceramic or
plastic container. Cover and refrigerate for 12–48 hours.

Rinse the duck legs and dry with paper towels. Melt the fat in a
large, deep saucepan over a low heat, and add the garlic, thyme and
duck legs. Cook the duck pieces in the fat over a very low heat for
2½–3 hours or until the meat is very soft. Transfer the duck legs to a
deep, non-metallic container and set aside to cool. When the fat has
cooled a little, strain and pour over the duck legs, making sure that
they are completely covered with the fat. Cover and refrigerate. The
confit may be stored this way for 2–3 months.

To serve, lift the duck pieces out of the fat and roast them in a 180°C
(350°F/Gas 4) oven for 15–20 minutes. Serve warm with lentils and
fried apple.

Crispy skin duck

Northern Chinese chefs have their famous Peking duck, but in Sichuan crispy skin duck is just as popular. Serve with Mandarin pancakes, available from Asian grocery stores.

Cooking time 1¾ hours
Serves 4

2.25 kg (5 lb) duck
8 spring onions (scallions), ends trimmed, smashed with flat side of a cleaver
8 slices fresh ginger, smashed with flat side of a cleaver
3 tablespoons Shaoxing rice wine
2 tablespoons salt
2 teaspoons Sichuan peppercorns
1 star anise, smashed with flat side of a cleaver
2 tablespoons light soy sauce
120 g (4½ oz) cornflour
oil for deep-frying
hoisin sauce
Mandarin pancakes

Rinse the duck, drain, and remove any fat from the cavity opening and around the neck. Cut off and discard the parson's nose (the fatty end of the tail). Combine the spring onion, ginger, rice wine, salt, peppercorns and star anise. Rub the marinade all over the inside and outside of the duck. Put the duck, breast-side-down, in a bowl with the remaining marinade and leave in the fridge for at least 1 hour. Put the duck and the marinade, breast-side-up, on a heatproof plate in a steamer, or cut into halves or quarters and put in several steamers.

Steam over simmering water in a covered wok for 1½ hours, replenishing with boiling water during cooking. Remove the duck and let it cool. Discard the marinade. Rub the soy sauce over the duck and then dredge in the cornflour, pressing lightly to make it adhere to the skin. Let the duck dry in the fridge for several hours until very dry.

Fill a wok one-quarter full of oil. Heat the oil to 190°C (375°F), or until a piece of bread fries golden brown in 10 seconds when dropped in the oil. Lower the duck into the oil and fry, ladling the oil over the top, until the skin is crisp and golden brown.

Drain the duck and, using a cleaver, cut it through the bones into pieces. Serve plain or with hoisin sauce and Mandarin pancakes.

Brandade de morue

This rich, garlicky purée is traditionally made with morue — salt cod.
Use a moist, centre-cut piece if you can.

Cooking time 30 minutes
Serves 4

750 g (1 lb 10 oz) piece salt cod
300 ml (10½ fl oz) olive oil
2 garlic cloves, crushed
300 ml (10½ fl oz) cream
2 tablespoons lemon juice
crispbreads

Put the salt cod in a shallow bowl and cover with cold water.
Refrigerate for 1–2 days, changing the water every 8 hours to
soak the salt out of the fish.

Drain the cod and rinse again. Put in a saucepan and cover with
2 litres (8 cups) of water. Bring to a simmer and cook for 10 minutes
(do not boil or the salt cod will toughen). Drain and rinse again.

Remove the skin and bones from the cod. Use a fork to flake the cod
into small pieces. Make sure there are no small bones left in the cod,
then finely chop in a food processor or with a sharp knife. (It will
have a fibrous texture.)

Heat 60 ml (2 fl oz) of the oil in a heavy-based frying pan and cook
the garlic over a low heat for 3 minutes without colouring. Add the
cod and stir in a spoonful of the remaining oil. Beat in a spoonful of
cream and continue adding the oil and cream alternately, beating
until the mixture is smooth and has the consistency of fluffy mashed
potato. Add the lemon juice and season with pepper (you won't need
to add any salt). Serve warm or cold with crispbread or toast. Keep in
the fridge for up to 3 days and warm through with a little extra
cream before serving.

Octopus in red wine stew

Ask your fishmonger to prepare the octopus for you if you're not sure how to do it, and watch and learn for the next time.

Cooking time 1 hour 10 minutes
Serves 4–6

1 kg (2 lb) baby octopus
2 tablespoons olive oil
1 large onion, chopped
3 garlic cloves, crushed
1 bay leaf
750 ml (3 cups) red wine
60 ml (¼ cup) red wine vinegar
400 g (14 oz) tin good-quality crushed tomatoes
1 tablespoon tomato paste (purée)
1 tablespoon finely chopped oregano
¼ teaspoon ground cinnamon
small pinch ground cloves
1 teaspoon sugar
2 tablespoons chopped flat-leaf (Italian) parsley

To prepare each octopus, take a small knife and cut between the head and tentacles, just below the eyes. Grasp the body and push the beak out and up through the centre of the tentacles with your fingers. Cut the eyes from the head by slicing a small round off with a small sharp knife. Discard the eye section. Carefully slit through one side of the head and remove any gut from inside. Thoroughly rinse the octopus under running water.

Heat the oil in a large saucepan, add the onion and cook over a high heat for 5 minutes, or until starting to brown. Add the garlic and bay leaf and cook for another minute. Add the octopus and stir to thoroughly coat in the onion mixture.

Add the wine, vinegar, tomato, tomato paste, oregano, cinnamon, cloves and sugar. Bring to the boil, then reduce the heat to low and simmer for 1 hour, or until the octopus is tender and the sauce has thickened slightly. Stir in the parsley and season.

Note: The cooking time for octopus varies according to the size. Generally the smaller octopus are not as tough as the larger ones and will take less time to cook.

Calamari ripieni

If your fishmonger has brought in a good catch of small tender squid, snap them up — this is the perfect recipe for them.

Cooking time 1¼ hours
Serves 4

600 g (1 lb 5 oz) small squid

Tomato sauce
800 g (1 lb 12 oz) tin chopped tomatoes
100 ml (3½ fl oz) red wine
2 tablespoons chopped flat-leaf (Italian) parsley
pinch sugar

Filling
100 ml (3½ fl oz) olive oil
1 small onion, finely chopped
1 small fennel bulb, finely chopped
2 garlic cloves, crushed
75 g (2½ oz) risotto rice
large pinch saffron threads
½ large red chilli, chopped
150 ml (5 fl oz) white wine
2 tablespoons chopped flat-leaf (Italian) parsley

Prepare the squid by pulling the heads and tentacles out of the bodies along with any innards. Cut the heads off below the eyes, just leaving the tentacles. Rinse the bodies, pulling out the transparent quills. Finely chop the tentacles and set aside with the squid bodies.

To make the tomato sauce, put the tomatoes, red wine, parsley and sugar in a saucepan. Season and simmer until some of the liquid has evaporated.

Heat the oil in a saucepan, add the onion, fennel and garlic and cook gently for 10 minutes until soft. Add the rice, saffron, chilli and chopped tentacles and cook for a few minutes, stirring frequently until the tentacles are opaque. Season, and add the white wine and 6 tablespoons of the tomato sauce. Cook, stirring frequently, until the tomato and wine have reduced into the rice. Add 150 ml (5 fl oz) of water and continue cooking until the rice is tender and all the liquid has been absorbed. Add the parsley and cool for a few minutes.

Stuff the squid with the filling, using a teaspoon to push the filling down to the bottom of the squid sacs. Do not overfill — you need to close the tops of the sacs easily without any filling squeezing out. Seal the tops with cocktail sticks.

Put the remaining tomato sauce in a saucepan with 200 ml (7 fl oz) of water. Cook for 2 minutes, then add the stuffed squid, cover the pan and simmer gently for 30–45 minutes, depending on the size of the squid, until soft and tender. Don't stir, or the filling may fall out (if a little filling does fall out it will merely add flavour to the sauce). Shake the pan slightly if you are worried about sticking.

Remove the cocktail sticks and serve the squid with a salad and some fresh bread.

Marmite dieppoise

This rich, soupy stew of shellfish and fish traditionally uses turbot and sole, but the salmon adds a splash of colour.

Cooking time 30 minutes
Serves 6

16 mussels
12 large prawns (shrimps)
450 ml (16 fl oz) cider or dry white wine
50 g (1¾ oz) butter
1 garlic clove, crushed
2 shallots (scallions), finely chopped
2 celery stalks, finely chopped
1 large leek, white part only, thinly sliced
250 g (9 oz) small chestnut mushrooms, sliced
1 bay leaf
300 g (10½ oz) salmon fillet, skinned and cut into chunks
400 g (14 oz) sole fillet, skinned and sliced widthways
300 ml (10½ fl oz) thick (double/heavy) cream
3 tablespoons finely chopped parsley

Scrub the mussels and remove their beards. Throw away any that are already open and don't close when tapped on the work surface. Peel and devein the prawns.

Pour the cider or white wine into a large saucepan and bring to a simmer. Add the mussels, cover the pan and cook for 3–5 minutes, shaking the pan every now and then. Put a fine sieve over a bowl and tip the mussels into the sieve. Transfer the mussels to a plate, throwing away any that haven't opened in the cooking time. Strain the cooking liquid again through the sieve, leaving behind any grit or sand. Clean the pan.

Add the butter to the cleaned saucepan and melt over a moderate heat. Add the garlic, shallot, celery and leek and cook for 7–10 minutes, or until the vegetables are just soft. Add the mushrooms and cook for a further 4–5 minutes, until softened. While the vegetables are cooking, remove the mussels from their shells.

Add the strained liquid to the vegetables in the saucepan, add the bay leaf and bring to a simmer. Add the salmon, sole and prawns and cook for 3–4 minutes until the fish is opaque and the prawns have turned pink. Stir in the cream and cooked mussels and simmer gently for 2 minutes. Season to taste and stir in the parsley.

Red vegetable curry

Nobody does vegetables quite like the Thais — so full of flavour the absence of meat is never an issue.

Cooking time 25–30 minutes
Serves 4

1 tablespoon oil
1 medium onion, chopped
1-2 tablespoons red curry paste
750 ml (2½ cups) coconut milk
4 Thai eggplants (aubergine), chopped
100 g (1 cup) bamboo shoots
6 makrut (kaffir) lime leaves
150 g (5½ oz) snake beans, cut into 3 cm (1 in) pieces
½ red capsicum (pepper), cut into strips
½ cup Thai basil leaves
2 tablespoons fish sauce
1 tablespoon lime juice
2 teaspoons palm sugar
1 large red chilli, sliced

Heat the oil in a large wok or frying pan. Cook the curry paste for 4 minutes over a medium heat, stirring.

Add the coconut milk, bring to the boil and simmer, uncovered, for 5 minutes. Add the eggplant, bamboo shoots and makrut lime leaves and simmer for 5 minutes. Add the snake beans and capsicum, and cook for 5 minutes or until the vegetables are tender.

Add the basil, fish sauce, lime juice and sugar. Drizzle with coconut milk and garnish with Thai basil and red chilli. Serve with steamed rice.

Spinach koftas in yoghurt sauce

This typical Gujarati dish is more substantial than many vegetarian dishes and is ideally served as part of an Indian buffet.

Cooking time 25 minutes
Serves 6

Yoghurt sauce
375 ml (13 fl oz) plain or Greek-style yoghurt
4 tablespoons besan (chickpea) flour
1 tablespoon oil
2 teaspoons black mustard seeds
1 teaspoon fenugreek seeds
6 curry leaves
1 large onion, finely chopped
3 garlic cloves, crushed
1 teaspoon ground turmeric
½ teaspoon chilli powder

Spinach koftas
1 bunch English spinach, leaves picked off the stems, or 500 g
(1 lb 2 oz) frozen spinach, thawed and drained
170 g besan (chickpea) flour
1 red onion, finely chopped
1 ripe tomato, finely diced
2 garlic cloves, crushed
1 teaspoon ground cumin
2 tablespoons coriander (cilantro) leaves
oil for deep-frying

To make the yoghurt sauce, whisk the yoghurt, besan flour and 750 ml (3 cups) of water in a large bowl until smooth. Heat the oil in a heavy-based saucepan or deep frying pan over a low heat. Add the mustard and fenugreek seeds and the curry leaves, cover and allow the seeds to pop for 1 minute. Add the onion and cook for 5 minutes, or until soft and starting to brown. Add the garlic and stir for 1 minute, or until soft. Add the turmeric and chilli powder and stir for 30 seconds. Add the yoghurt mixture, bring to the boil and simmer over a low heat for 10 minutes. Season with salt.

To make the spinach koftas, blanch the spinach in boiling water for 1 minute and refresh in cold water. Drain, squeezing out any extra water by putting the spinach between two plates and pushing them together. Finely chop the spinach. Combine with the remaining kofta ingredients and up to 60 ml (¼ cup) of water, a little at a time, adding enough to make the mixture soft but not sloppy. If it becomes too sloppy, add more besan flour. Season with salt, to taste. (To test the seasoning, fry a small amount of the mixture and taste it.) Shape the mixture into balls by rolling it in dampened hands, using 1 tablespoon of mixture for each.

Fill a heavy-based saucepan one-third full with oil and heat to 180°C/350°F (a cube of bread will brown in 15 seconds). Lower the koftas into the oil in batches and fry until golden and crisp. Don't overcrowd the pan. Remove the koftas as they cook, shake off any excess oil and add them to the yoghurt sauce.

Gently reheat the yoghurt sauce, and if you like, sprinkle with the coriander leaves just before serving.

In the oven

What could be easier than an oven-cooked meal that has bubbled away at a leisurely pace, producing intense flavours and food so tender you could eat it with a spoon? Not only tasty, but also deliciously simple.

Slow-roasted beef with beets and horseradish cream

With a good proportion of fat, beef forerib is a wonderful cut of meat for slow roasting as it remains moist and succulent. Sweet and tender roast beetroot makes the perfect partner.

Cooking time 2½–3 hours
Serves 6–8

2 large onions
3–3½ kg (about 6 lb 8 oz) piece forerib of beef on the bone/standing rib roast
100 g (3½ oz) butter, softened
3 tablespoons Dijon mustard
10 sprigs thyme
1 tablespoon plain (all-purpose) flour
8 medium beetroot

Horseradish cream
50 g (1¾ oz) peeled fresh horseradish, soaked in cold water for 1 hour
1 teaspoon caster (superfine) sugar
½ teaspoon dry mustard
2 teaspoons white wine vinegar
150 ml (5 fl oz) cream

Preheat the oven to 230°C (450°F/Gas 8). Peel and cut the onions into 6–7 slices each. Set aside 8 of the smaller slices, then put the rest in the centre of a large baking pan.

Blend the butter, mustard and 2 sprigs of chopped thyme together until smooth. Season with a little salt and plenty of freshly ground black pepper. Wipe the meat well with damp paper towels. Rub all over with half of the mustard butter and put fatty-side-up on the onions in the pan. Sprinkle the flour over the top.

Clean the beetroot but do not peel. Cut a shallow cross in the top of each and put on a reserved onion ring. Position around the beef. Spoon ¼ teaspoon of the remaining mustard butter on top of each. Reserve the unused butter. Transfer the pan to the oven and roast uncovered for 20 minutes. Reduce the temperature to 160°C (315°F/Gas 2–3) and roast for a further 35 minutes per kilogram (2 lb 4 oz). Add an extra 20 minutes at the end for medium, and 35 minutes for well done. Baste the beef and beets every 30 minutes.

Turn the oven off. Put another dob of mustard butter on each beetroot, and top this with a sprig of thyme. Spread the last of the butter over the top of the roast. Return to the oven, prop the door open and leave to rest for 15 minutes.

To make the horseradish cream, dry the horseradish thoroughly and grate very finely. Mix with the sugar, mustard and vinegar. Whip the cream until it forms stiff peaks. Fold in the other ingredients and season to taste with salt and pepper. Spoon into a serving bowl.

Carve the beef and put the slices on a warm platter. Top with the onion slices from the bottom of the pan, and arrange the beets around the edges (cut them into smaller pieces if you prefer). Serve the horseradish cream separately.

Note • Have the butcher chine the joint (cut through the tip of the vertebrae within the joint) to make carving easier, and cap the ends of the exposed ribs with foil to stop them burning during cooking.

Beef in Barolo

Barolo, the famous red wine from Piedmont in Italy's north west, is known as 'the king of wines and the wine of kings'. It is the perfect wine for slow-cooking beef.

Cooking time 4¼ hours
Serves 6–8

Marinade
750 ml (1 bottle) Barolo
1 carrot, coarsely chopped
1 onion, coarsely chopped
1 celery stalk, coarsely chopped
6 sprigs parsley
1 sprig rosemary
1 sprig sage
2 bay leaves
10 black peppercorns
2 garlic cloves, bruised with the flat blade of a knife

1½ kg (3 lb 5 oz) piece of beef rump
50 g (1¾ oz) pork fat, cut into thin strips
¼ teaspoon nutmeg
2 tablespoons plain (all-purpose) flour
3 tablespoons olive oil
3 tablespoons butter
1 onion, sliced
125 ml (½ cup) brandy

For the marinade, pour the wine into a non-metallic bowl and add the carrot, onion, celery, parsley, rosemary, sage, bay leaves, peppercorns and garlic. Make deep incisions all over the beef using the point of a thin sharp knife, then push in the strips of pork fat. Tie the beef up salami-fashion with kitchen string and put in the marinade. Cover and refrigerate for at least 6 hours, turning once or twice.

Preheat the oven to 170°C (325°F/gas 3). Remove the beef and dry with paper towels. Rub all over with the nutmeg, flour and salt and pepper. Heat the oil and butter in a large flameproof casserole dish or stockpot. Brown the beef over a medium heat for 8–10 minutes. Add the sliced onion and soften over a low heat for 5 minutes. Pour in the brandy, increase the heat and cook until it evaporates. Pour in the marinade and bring to the boil. Cover with a double sheet of foil and put the lid on. Cook in the oven for 3½–4 hours, or until the beef is fork tender and juicy. Turn it occasionally.

Transfer the beef to a carving tray and cover with foil to keep warm. Discard the herbs from the sauce. Purée in a processor, or put it through a food mill. Return to the pot and bring to the boil. Taste for seasoning. Cut the string off the beef and carve it thickly. Serve with the sauce spooned over the top. Silverbeet (Swiss chard) tossed in butter makes a good accompaniment.

Beef cooked in ragù

This dish is a starter and main course in one pot. Serve the ragù on pasta as a starter, and the beef with vegetables or a salad for the main course.

Cooking time 2 hours
Serves 6

1 x 1.5 kg (3 lb 5 oz) piece of beef, such as top rump or silverside
60 g (2¼ oz) pork fat, cut into small thin pieces
30 g (1 oz) butter
3 tablespoons olive oil
pinch cayenne pepper
2 garlic cloves, finely chopped
2 onions, finely chopped
2 carrots, finely chopped
1 celery stalk, finely chopped
½ red capsicum (pepper), finely chopped
3 leeks, sliced
185 ml (¾ cup) red wine
1 tablespoon tomato paste (purée)
375 ml (13 fl oz) beef stock
200 ml (7 fl oz) tomato passata
8 basil leaves, torn into pieces
½ teaspoon finely chopped oregano leaves
2 tablespoons finely chopped parsley
60 ml (¼ cup) thick (double/heavy) cream
roasted onions

Make deep incisions all over the beef with the point of a sharp knife, then push a piece of pork fat into each incision.

Heat the butter and olive oil in a large casserole dish and brown the beef for 10–12 minutes, until it is browned all over. Season with salt and add the cayenne, garlic, onion, carrot, celery, pepper and leek. Cook over a moderate heat for 10 minutes until the vegetables are lightly browned.

Increase the heat, add the wine and boil until it has evaporated. Stir in the tomato paste, then add the stock. Simmer for 30 minutes. Add the passata, basil and oregano and season with pepper. Cover the casserole and cook for about 1 hour, or until the beef is tender.

Remove the beef from the casserole and allow to rest for 10 minutes before carving. Taste the sauce for salt and pepper and stir in the parsley and cream. Serve with roasted onions.

Beef carbonade

This Belgian dish gets its rich colour from dark Flemish beer. It has a faint caramel aroma and flavour.

Cooking time 3 hours
Serves 6–8

½ tablespoon butter
150 g (5½ oz) speck or slab bacon, cubed
1 kg (2 lb 4 oz) onions, thinly sliced
1 tablespoon brown sugar
60 g (½ cup) plain (all-purpose) flour
2 kg (4 lb 8 oz) chuck steak, cubed
80 ml (⅓ cup) red wine vinegar
1 litre (4 cups) Flemish beer, or other dark beer
2 teaspoons thyme leaves
2 bay leaves
2 thick slices fresh bread, crusts removed
3 tablespoons strong mustard
4 tablespoons chopped parsley

Melt the butter in a large frying pan and fry the speck over a medium heat until it is browned and the fat is rendered. Remove with a slotted spoon and reserve. Add the onions to the fat and cook slowly, covered, for 20 minutes. Uncover, increase the heat and stir the sugar through. Cook, stirring, until caramelized. Transfer to a strainer set over a bowl. Press with the back of a spoon to extract excess fat. Transfer the onions to a large earthenware casserole dish and reserve the fat. Preheat the oven to 160°C (315°F/Gas 2–3).

Season the flour well with salt and pepper. Toss the beef in the flour and coat well. Brown the beef in batches over a high heat, adding a little of the reserved fat if needed. As each batch is done, transfer to the casserole dish. Add the red wine vinegar to the pan and deglaze. Add 250 ml (1 cup) of beer and bring to the boil. Transfer to the casserole dish along with the speck. Add the thyme and bay leaves and stir to combine the contents.

Pour in enough of the remaining beer to barely reach the surface. Thickly spread one side of the bread slices with mustard and put side by side on top of the beef, mustard-side-down. Cover the dish with a double thickness of foil, sealing the edges well, then put the lid on and bake for 2 hours.

Discard the bread and taste for seasoning. Add three-quarters of the parsley and gently turn the contents over. Sprinkle the remaining parsley on top for serving.

Boeuf en croûte

For this dish to work really well, ask the butcher for a piece of centre-cut beef fillet that is an even thickness all the way along. This is also called Beef Wellington.

Cooking time 1 hour
Serves 6

Pâté
180 g (6 oz) butter
3 shallots (scallions), chopped
1 garlic clove, chopped
360 g (12 oz) chicken livers
1 tablespoon brandy or Cognac

1 kg (2 lb 4 oz) thick beef fillet
30 g (1 oz) dripping or butter
600 g (1 lb 5 oz) puff pastry
1 egg, lightly beaten

To make the pâté, melt half the butter in a frying pan and add shallots and garlic. Cook until softened but not browned.

Remove any discoloured spots from the chicken livers, wash and pat dry. Add the chicken livers to the frying pan and sauté for 4–5 minutes, or until cooked but still a little pink in the middle. Let the livers cool completely and then process in a food processor with the rest of the butter and the brandy. Alternatively, push the chopped livers through a sieve and mix with the butter and brandy. Season.

Preheat the oven to 220°C (425°F/Gas 7). Tie the beef four or five times along its length to keep it in shape. Heat the dripping in a roasting tin and brown the beef on all sides, then put in the oven and roast for 20 minutes. Allow to cool and remove the string.

Reduce the oven temperature to 200°C (400°F/Gas 6). Roll the pastry into a rectangle just big enough to cover the beef fillet completely. Trim the edges and keep them for decoration. Spread the pâté over the pastry, leaving a border around the edge. Brush the border with beaten egg.

Lay the fillet on the pastry and wrap it up tightly like a parcel, pressing the seams together firmly and tucking the ends under. Put the parcel, seam-side-down, on a baking tray and brush all over with beaten egg. Cut pieces from the trimmings to decorate the pastry and brush with beaten egg. Bake for 25–30 minutes for rare and 35–40 minutes for medium. Allow the beef to rest for 5 minutes before carving.

Boeuf bourguignon

This well-known dish from Burgundy, France, is best made a day in advance to allow the flavours to develop fully.

Cooking time 3¼ hours
Serves 6

1.5 kg (3 lb 5 oz) beef blade or chuck steak
750 ml (1 bottle) red wine (preferably Burgundy)
3 garlic cloves, crushed
bouquet garni
70 g (2½ oz) butter
1 onion, chopped
1 carrot, chopped
2 tablespoons plain (all-purpose) flour
200 g (7 oz) bacon, cut into short strips
300 g (10½ oz) French shallots, peeled
200 g (7 oz) small button mushrooms

Cut the meat into small cubes and trim away any excess fat. Put the meat, wine, garlic and bouquet garni in a large bowl, cover with plastic wrap and leave in the fridge for at least 3 hours and preferably overnight.

Preheat the oven to 160°C (315°F/Gas 2–3). Drain the meat, reserving the marinade and bouquet garni. Dry the meat on paper towels. Heat 30 g (1 oz) of the butter in a large casserole dish. Add the onion, carrot and bouquet garni and cook over a low heat, stirring occasionally, for 10 minutes. Remove from the heat.

Heat half of the remaining butter in a large frying pan over a high heat. Fry the meat in batches for about 5 minutes or until well browned. Add to the casserole dish.

Pour the reserved marinade into the frying pan and boil, stirring, for 30 seconds to deglaze the pan. Remove from the heat. Return the casserole to high heat and sprinkle the meat and vegetables with the flour. Cook, stirring constantly, until the meat is well coated with the flour. Pour in the marinade and stir well. Bring to the boil, stirring constantly, then cover and cook in the oven for 2 hours.

Heat the remaining butter in the clean frying pan and cook the bacon and shallots, stirring, for 8–10 minutes or until the shallots are softened but not browned. Add the mushrooms and cook, stirring occasionally, for 2–3 minutes or until browned. Drain on paper towels. Add the shallots, bacon and mushrooms to the casserole.

Cover the casserole and return to the oven for 30 minutes, or until the meat is soft and tender. Discard the bouquet garni. Season to taste and skim any fat from the surface before serving.

Cottage pie

A variation on shepherd's pie which uses lamb, the hearty, unbeatable combination of beef and mash makes this a British favourite.

Cooking time 2 hours
Serves 6–8

3 tablespoons dripping or olive oil
2 onions, finely sliced
2 garlic cloves, crushed
2 carrots, chopped
1 kg (2 lb 4 oz) minced (ground) beef
2 tablespoons plain (all-purpose) flour
375 ml (1½ cups) beef stock
1 tablespoon tomato paste (purée)
1 tablespoon Worcestershire sauce
1 teaspoon chopped thyme
1 tablespoon chopped parsley
¼ teaspoon ground cinnamon
1 bay leaf
900 g (2 lb) desiree or mashing potatoes
75 g (2½ oz) butter
1 tablespoon milk

Heat 2 tablespoons Of dripping or oil in a large saucepan and cook the onions, garlic and carrots over a moderate heat for 7–10 minutes or until softened. Set aside. Add the remaining oil to a frying pan, add the beef and cook for 7–10 minutes or until lightly coloured, stirring and breaking up any clumps that form. Sprinkle with the flour, stir and cook for a further minute.

Add the stock, tomato paste, Worcestershire sauce, herbs and cinnamon and bring to the boil. Transfer to the large saucepan and add the onions. Add the bay leaf, bring to the boil, and gently simmer over a low heat for 45 minutes. Add a little more stock if the mixture becomes dry. Set aside to cool.

Peel the potatoes and cut them into 3 cm (1 in) pieces. Put in a large saucepan of salted water and bring to the boil. Cook over a moderate heat for 15–20 minutes or until soft. Drain, return to the pan, and add the butter and mash with a little milk. The mash needs to remain firm. Beat with a wooden spoon to aerate it and make it fluffy.

Preheat the oven to 180°C (350°F/Gas 4). Lightly grease a 2.5 litre (10 cup) ovenproof dish. Spoon the filling into the dish and spread the mash over the top. Fluff the mash with a fork and bake for 30–35 minutes or until the topping is golden and the filling is bubbling.

Lasagne al forno

This multi-layered dish is traditionally made with lasagne verde, but plain pasta will do if you prefer.

Cooking time 3½ hours
Serves 6

Meat sauce
30 g (1 oz) butter
1 onion, finely chopped
1 small carrot, finely chopped
½ celery stalk, finely chopped
1 garlic clove, crushed
120 g (4½ oz) pancetta, sliced
500 g (1 lb 2 oz) minced (ground) beef
¼ teaspoon dried oregano
pinch nutmeg
90 g (3¼ oz) chicken livers, trimmed and finely chopped
75 ml (⅓ cup) dry vermouth or dry white wine
350 ml (12 fl oz) beef stock
1 tablespoon tomato paste (purée)
2 tablespoons thick (double/heavy) cream
1 egg, beaten

Béchamel sauce
65 g (2½ oz) butter
40 g (1½ oz) plain (all-purpose) flour
pinch grated nutmeg
625 ml (2½ cups) milk
1 bay leaf
125 ml (½ cup) thick (double/heavy) cream

6 sheets fresh lasagne verde or 6 sheets dried lasagne
150 g (5½ oz) mozzarella cheese, grated
60 g (2¼ oz) Parmesan cheese, grated

To make the meat sauce, heat the butter in a frying pan and add the vegetables, garlic and pancetta. Cook over a moderately low heat for 5–6 minutes, or until softened. Add the beef, increase the heat a little and cook for 8 minutes, or until coloured but not browned, stirring to break up the lumps. Add the oregano and nutmeg and season well.

Stir in the chicken livers and cook until they change colour. Pour in the vermouth, increase the heat and cook until it has evaporated. Add the beef stock and tomato paste and simmer for 2 hours. Add a little hot water, if necessary, during this time to keep the mixture moist, but towards the end let all the liquid be absorbed. Stir in the cream, remove from the heat and leave to cool for 15 minutes. Stir in the egg.

To make the béchamel sauce, heat the butter in a saucepan over a low heat. Add the flour and nutmeg and cook, stirring, for 1 minute. Remove from the heat and gradually stir in the milk. Add the bay leaf, return to the heat and simmer, stirring often, until the sauce thickens. Season, cover with plastic wrap to prevent a skin forming, and cool. Discard the bay leaf.

Put the béchamel in a saucepan, heat gently and stir in the cream. Remove from the heat and cool slightly. Preheat the oven to 180°C (350°F/Gas 4) and grease a 22 x 15 x 7 cm (8½ x 6 x 2½ in) ovenproof dish.

If using fresh pasta, cut it into manageable sheets. Cook the pasta in batches in a large saucepan of boiling salted water until al dente. Scoop out each batch with a slotted spoon as it is done and drop into a bowl of cold water. Spread the sheets out in a single layer on a tea towel, turning them over once to blot dry each side. Trim any torn edges.

Spread half the meat sauce in the dish. Scatter with half the mozzarella, then cover with a slightly overlapping layer of pasta sheets. Spread half the béchamel over this and sprinkle with half the Parmesan. Repeat the layers, finishing with a layer of béchamel and Parmesan.

Bake for about 40 minutes until golden brown and leave to rest for 10 minutes before serving.

Pork with apples

A splash of Calvados, an apple brandy distilled from cider, transforms traditional apple sauce from the ordinary to the sublime.

Cooking time 1¾ hours
Serves 8

1.8 kg (4 lb) joint of pork with the skin on
6 garlic cloves
12 baby onions
16 baby apples or 4 Golden Delicious, peeled and quartered
60 g (2¼ oz) butter
2 teaspoons brown sugar
1 tablespoon Calvados
2 tablespoons crème fraîche

Preheat the oven to 180°C (350°F/Gas 4). Remove the skin from the pork and trim off some of the fat, leaving on a thin covering. Score the outside of the skin in a criss-cross pattern using a sharp knife, but don't cut all the way through. Tie the skin back on the joint and rub it with salt. Season the underside of the meat and put the joint, bone-side-down, in a roasting tin with the garlic cloves and onions.

Roast for 1½ hours, or until cooked through. To test the inner temperature, push a skewer into the meat and pull it out after a few seconds — if it feels very hot the meat will be cooked through. Rest the meat for 15 minutes before carving, keeping the garlic and onions warm. If you want to make the crackling crisper, remove it and and crisp it under a hot grill (broiler). Pour any meat juices into a jug and skim off the fat.

Sauté the apples in butter in a frying pan for a minute, then add the sugar and increase the heat. Cook the apples until caramelized. Remove and keep warm. Add the Calvados to the pan and cook for a minute, then add the meat juices and crème fraîche and stir to make a gravy. Serve the pork with the apples, onions and garlic, and pass the gravy around.

Florentine roast pork

Everyone loves a roast dinner, and most families have a treasured recipe that's handed down through the generations. Here's a delectable Italian version.

Cooking time 1¾ hours
Serves 6

3 large fennel bulbs
½ tablespoon finely chopped rosemary
4 garlic cloves, crushed
1 x 1.5 kg (3 lb 5 oz) pork loin, chined and skinned
3 white onions
80 ml (⅓ cup) olive oil
185 ml (¾ cup) dry white wine
80 ml (⅓ cup) extra virgin olive oil
250 ml (1 cup) chicken stock
3–4 tablespoons thick (double/heavy) cream

Preheat the oven to 200°C (400°F/Gas 6). Cut the green fronds from the tops of the fennel and chop to give 2 tablespoons. Mix with the rosemary, garlic and plenty of salt and black pepper. Make deep incisions with a sharp knife all over the pork and rub this mixture into the incisions and the splits in the pork bone. Cut two of the onions in half and put in a roasting tin. Put the pork on top of the onion and drizzle the olive oil over the top.

Roast in the oven for 30 minutes. Baste the pork with the pan juices, then reduce the temperature to 180°C (350°F/Gas 4). Roast for a further 30 minutes. Baste and lightly salt the surface of the pork. Pour in half the white wine. Continue roasting for another 30–45 minutes, basting once or twice.

Meanwhile, remove the tough outer leaves of the fennel and discard. Slice the bulbs vertically into thin sections and put in a large saucepan. Thinly slice the remaining onion and add to the saucepan with the extra virgin olive oil and a little salt. Add enough water to cover, put the lid on and bring to the boil. Simmer for about 45 minutes, or until the fennel is creamy and soft and almost all the liquid has evaporated.

Remove the pork from the tin and leave to rest in a warm spot. Spoon off the excess oil from the tin and discard the onion. Put the tin over a high heat on the stovetop and stir in the remaining wine to deglaze. Add the stock and boil the sauce until slightly thickened. Remove from the heat, season with salt and pepper and stir in the cream. Slice the pork and serve on the fennel, with the sauce.

Baked Southern-style sticky ribs

These ribs are sweet, spicy and tender with just a hint of smokiness.

Cooking time 3½ hours
Serves 6

2 large onions, thickly sliced
2 bay leaves
1 teaspoon black peppercorns
12 rashers bacon
2 kg (4 lb 8 oz) meaty pork spare ribs, cut into serving size portions of 3–4 ribs

Glaze
2½ tablespoons Worcestershire sauce
2 tablespoons American mustard
juice of 1 small orange
2 tablespoons cider vinegar
2 tablespoons bourbon
1½ tablespoons molasses
¾ cup muscavado sugar
3 tablespoons tomato paste (purée)
4 garlic cloves, crushed
½ teaspoon Tabasco
freshly ground black pepper
1 teaspoon salt
small pinch ground cloves

Preheat oven to 150°C (300°F/Gas 2) . Put the onions, bay leaves and peppercorns in the base of a large roasting tin, lay the ribs on top, then evenly cover with a single layer of 6 bacon rashers. Pour over 750 ml (3 cups) of water. Cover the tin tightly with foil so the steam cannot escape, then cook in the preheated oven for 2 hours and 45 minutes.

Remove from the oven. Increase the temperature to 180°C (350°F/Gas 4). Combine the remaining glaze ingredients in a small saucepan, whisk until smooth, then bring to the boil, stirring occasionally, for 2 minutes. Remove from the heat.

Peel off the bacon and discard. Divide the remaining 6 bacon rashers over the base of two foil-lined roasting tins or oven trays. Discard the onions and pan juices, or strain the mixture, skim off all the fat and serve the tasty broth in small cups alongside the ribs, if desired. Liberally brush each rib all over with the glaze, then put in a single layer over the top of the bacon and cook, uncovered, for a further 45 minutes, brushing regularly with the glaze until the meat is very tender and the glaze is sticky.

Give the ribs one last brush with the glaze. Serve them with the bacon, accompanied by baked potatoes and sour cream.

Navarin of lamb

A navarin is simply a lamb stew cooked with root vegetables. It's the sort of all-in-one dish that's guaranteed to satisfy the healthiest of appetites.

Cooking time 3 hours
Serves 8

1.25 kg (2 lb 12 oz) lamb, boned shoulder or leg meat
4 tablespoons vegetable oil
1 tablespoon plain (all-purpose) flour
500 ml (2 cups) lamb stock
2 tablespoons tomato paste (purée)
750 ml (3 cups) lamb stock
3 rashers bacon, chopped
2 carrots, roughly chopped
1 onion, chopped
3 garlic cloves, crushed
1 leek, roughly chopped
10 spring onions (scallions), stems removed
1 tablespoon thyme
700 g (1 lb 9 oz) desiree potatoes, peeled and sliced

Preheat the oven to 160°C (315°F/Gas 2–3). Trim the lamb and cut into 5 cm (2 in) pieces. Heat 2 tablespoons of oil in a large frying pan and cook the lamb over a moderate heat until brown, turning occasionally. Don't overload the pan — this may have to be done in two stages. Sprinkle with flour, stir well and gradually add the stock and the tomato paste. Stir well, cook for 1 minute until thickened and put in the bottom of a large flameproof casserole dish. Heat the remaining oil and cook the bacon, onions, carrots, garlic and leek, stirring regularly until the onions are lightly browned. Add to the casserole dish.

Add the spring onions and thyme to the dish, cover, and bake for 1 hour. Uncover the casserole dish and skim the fat from the surface. Season with a little salt and pepper and push the sliced potatoes into the dish, covering the surface with a thick layer. Replace the lid and bake for a further 45 minutes or until the potatoes are tender. Turn the oven up to 180°C (350°F/Gas 4), remove the lid and cook for another 25 minutes or until the potatoes are golden. If you like, serve with steamed green beans.

Lamb shanks with tomato, chilli and honey

Lamb shanks are well suited to long, slow cooking. The spices in this recipe are dry-roasted before the meat is cooked for added depth of flavour.

Cooking time 2¾ hours
Serves 4

6 lamb shanks, each weighing 275 g (9¾ oz)
1 small red capsicum (pepper), cut into chunks
1 small orange capsicum (pepper), cut into chunks
1 small yellow capsicum (pepper), cut into chunks
4 garlic cloves, cut into slivers
2 brown onions, peeled and chopped
750 ml (1 bottle) full-bodied red wine, such as Shiraz
1 tablespoon cumin seeds
1½ tablespoons coriander seeds
2 tablespoons olive oil
2 red chillies, deseeded and finely chopped
400 g (14 oz) tin chopped tomatoes
3 tablespoons honey
1 tablespoon plain (all-purpose) flour

Put the lamb shanks into a large plastic container or dish. Add the capsicum, garlic and onion and pour the red wine over the top. Cover and leave to marinate for a few hours or overnight in the refrigerator.

Put the cumin seeds in a frying pan over a medium heat. Stir while they toast for 2–3 minutes — they will start to smell aromatic and jump in the pan when ready. Tip them into a mortar, then dry-roast the coriander seeds. Grind the spices to a powder.

Lift the lamb shanks out of the marinade. Strain the rest of the marinade ingredients, reserving the liquid. Heat the oil in a flameproof casserole dish and, when hot, brown the shanks in batches. Transfer to a plate and remove all but 1 tablespoon of the fat. Preheat the oven to 180°C (350°F/Gas 4).

Add the reserved vegetables and chilli to the casserole dish and cook for 8–10 minutes or until the onion has softened a little. Meanwhile, mix the chopped tomatoes and honey into the marinade liquid.

Scatter the ground spices and flour over the vegetables and stir. Pour in the marinade mixture and stir everything together. Season with salt. Add the lamb shanks and bring the liquid to the boil. Cover with a lid and transfer to the oven for 2 hours. Turn the shanks halfway through cooking.

Transfer the shanks to a large, deep serving dish and keep warm. Put the liquid over direct heat and bring to the boil. Bubble for 10 minutes to reduce the sauce. Pour the sauce over the meat and garnish with coriander, if you like.

Mechoui

Mechoui is a spicy Moroccan dish of tender, slow-roasted lamb that is basted with a cumin and paprika paste as it cooks.

Cooking time 3½ hours
Serves 6

2.2 kg (5 lb) leg of lamb
75 g (3 oz) butter, softened at room temperature
3 garlic cloves, crushed
2 teaspoons ground cumin
3 teaspoons ground coriander
1 teaspoon paprika
1 tablespoon ground cumin, for dipping

Preheat the oven to hot 220°C (425°F/Gas 7). With a sharp knife, cut small deep slits in the top and sides of the lamb.

Mix the butter, garlic, spices and ¼ teaspoon of salt in a bowl until a smooth paste forms.

With the back of a spoon rub the paste all over the lamb, then use your fingers to spread the paste and make sure all the lamb is covered.

Put the lamb bone–side–down in a deep baking dish and put on the top shelf of the oven. Bake for 10 minutes, then baste and return to the oven. Reduce the temperature to 150°C (300°F/Gas 2). Bake for 3 hours and 20 minutes, basting every 20–30 minutes to make the lamb flavoursome and tender. Carve the lamb into chunky pieces. Mix the cumin with 1½ teaspoons salt and serve on the side for dipping.

Gigot d'agneau

Tender enough to be eaten with a spoon, this slow-cooked lamb is bound to be the best you have ever tasted.

Cooking time 5 hours
Serves 6

2 kg (4 lb 8 oz) leg of lamb
750 ml (1 bottle) dry red wine
60 ml (¼ cup) brandy
20 garlic cloves, bruised
1 tablespoon chopped rosemary leaves
2 teaspoons chopped thyme leaves
2 bay leaves, torn into small pieces
1 large carrot, diced
1 large celery stalk, diced
1 onion, finely chopped
60 ml (¼ cup) olive oil
1 tablespoon olive oil, for browning
1 tablespoon butter
1¼ litres (5 cups) lamb or chicken stock

Trim any really thick pieces of fat from the lamb but leave it with a decent covering all over if possible. Combine the wine, brandy, garlic, herbs, vegetables and oil in a non-metallic baking dish, then add the lamb and turn to coat. Cover and refrigerate for 24–48 hours, turning occasionally so the marinade is evenly distributed. Wrap and re-wrap the dish tightly with plastic wrap each time to ensure strong odours from the marinade do not permeate other foods in the fridge.

Preheat the oven to 120°C (250°F/Gas ½). Allow the lamb to come to room temperature before removing from the marinade. Reserve the marinade, and blot up any excess liquid from the leg with paper towels. Heat the olive oil and butter in a sturdy roasting tin over a medium heat, add the lamb and brown all over. Add the marinade to the base of the tin with enough stock to bring the liquid level halfway up the lamb. Lightly cover with foil. Put in the oven and cook, basting regularly with the stock at least every half hour or so for 4 hours. Remove the foil and continue to cook and baste for a further hour or until the meat is very tender and almost falling off the bone.

Carefully transfer the lamb to a serving platter. Cover with foil, then a tea towel to keep it warm while you make the sauce. Whiz all the ingredients left in the pan in a food processor, then strain the liquid into a large saucepan and boil until it is reduced to 375 ml (1½ cups) and has thickened slightly. Carve the lamb and serve with the sauce and a potato gratin.

Moussaka

Moussaka is a Greek staple in home kitchens and tavernas alike. Each step of preparation brings out the best from the ingredients so that when they are layered together a rich and luscious dish emerges.

Cooking time 5 hours
Serves 6

250 ml (1 cup) olive oil
3 large yellow capsicums (peppers), finely chopped
1 kg (2 lb 4 oz) minced (ground) lamb
2 large onions, finely chopped
3 garlic cloves, crushed
½ teaspoon nutmeg
¼ teaspoon ground allspice
200 ml (7 fl oz) dry red wine
800 g (1 lb 12 oz) tin chopped tomatoes
75 g (2½ oz) currants
1 kg (2 lb 4 oz) eggplant (aubergine), cut into thin slices
600 g (1 lb 5 oz) potatoes, peeled
4 tablespoons grated kefalotyri or Parmesan cheese
4 tablespoons chopped parsley
500 g (1 lb 2 oz) Greek–style yoghurt
2 egg yolks
150 g (5½ oz) fresh mozzarella cheese, grated

Heat 2 tablespoons of the oil in a large frying pan. Add the capsicum and cook over a moderately low heat for 7–8 minutes until soft. Remove from the pan and reserve. Heat 2 tablespoons of oil in the pan, increase the heat and add the lamb. Sauté until it changes colour (about 8 minutes). Break up any lumps with the back of the spoon as you stir.

Add the onions and garlic and cook for a further 10 minutes. Stir in the nutmeg and allspice and cook for 1 minute. Add the wine, tomatoes and currants. Reduce the heat to low, cover and simmer for 2 hours. Stir occasionally, and add hot water 3–4 tablespoons at a time, if the sauce dries out. When cooked, it should be thick with very little liquid left. Season to taste.

Meanwhile, heat a griddle or barbecue grill to hot. Brush the eggplant with lots of oil and grill for 8–10 minutes until golden brown on both sides. Reserve. Put the potatoes in a saucepan and cover with hot water. Bring to the boil. Reduce the heat and simmer for 5 minutes. Drain and rinse under cold water. Cut into thin slices and reserve.

Preheat the oven to 170°C (325°F/Gas 3) and grease a 30 x 20 x 5 cm (12 x 8 x 2 in) earthenware ovenproof dish. Using the potato slices, cover the bottom of the dish in a slightly overlapping layer. Season with pepper and sprinkle 2 tablespoons of the kefalotyri over the top. Arrange half of the eggplant slices over this. Stir the parsley into the lamb sauce and spread half over the eggplant. Now spread the capsicum on top and sprinkle with 2 tablespoons of kefalotyri. Spread over the remaining sauce and smooth the surface. Cover with foil and bake for 2 hours.

Beat the yoghurt and egg yolks together until smooth. Spread over the moussaka, completely covering the surface. Layer the remaining eggplant slices over this and sprinkle with the last of the kefalotyri. Scatter the mozzarella over the surface. Return to the oven uncovered for 30 minutes, or until the top is just beginning to brown. Remove from the oven and rest for 10 minutes. Cut into squares to serve.

Roast chicken

Once served as the traditional Sunday lunch, roast chicken is currently undergoing a revival as the sort of meal to be enjoyed by the whole family.

Cooking time 1¼ hours
Serves 4

45 g (1½ oz) butter, softened
1 x 1.6 kg (3 lb 8 oz) chicken
1 sprig tarragon or rosemary
2 onions, quartered
300 ml (10½ fl oz) chicken stock

Preheat the oven to 200°C (400°F/Gas 6). Place half the butter inside the chicken with the tarragon or rosemary and onion. Rub the chicken with the remaining butter and season. Tie the legs together and tuck the wing tips under. Put the chicken, breast-side-down, in a roasting tin and add the stock.

Cover the chicken loosely with foiL and roast for 30 minutes, basting occasionally. Uncover, turn the chicken and roast for 30–40 minutes, or until golden brown and the juices run clear when the thigh is pierced with a skewer.

Remove the chicken from the tin, cover with foil and a tea towel and leave to rest. Put the tin on the stovetop and skim off most of the fat. Boil rapidly until the juices reduce and become syrupy. Strain and serve with the chicken.

Chicken with 40 cloves of garlic

Roasted garlic mellows and sweetens while it bakes, so when you come to serve it, you're left with a delicious creamy flesh that oozes out of its skin.

Cooking time 1 hour 25 minutes
Serves 4

2 celery stalks, including leaves
2 sprigs rosemary
4 sprigs thyme
4 sprigs flat-leaf (Italian) parsley
1 x 1.6 kg (3 lb 8 oz) chicken
40 garlic cloves, unpeeled
2 tablespoons olive oil
1 carrot, roughly chopped
1 small onion, cut into 4 wedges
250 ml (1 cup) white wine
1 baguette, cut into slices

Preheat the oven to 200°C (400°F/Gas 6). Put a chopped celery stalk and 2 sprigs each of the rosemary, thyme and parsley into the chicken cavity. Add 6 cloves of garlic. Tie the legs together and tuck the wing tips under.

Brush the chicken liberally with some of the oil and season well. Scatter about 10 more garlic cloves over the base of a large casserole dish. Put the remaining sprigs of herbs, chopped celery, carrot and onion in the casserole dish.

Put the chicken in the dish. Scatter the remaining garlic cloves around the chicken and add the remaining oil and the wine. Cover and bake for 1 hour 20 minutes, or until the chicken is tender and the juices run clear when the thigh is pierced with a skewer.

To serve, carefully lift the chicken out of the casserole dish. Strain off the juices into a small saucepan. Use tongs to pick out the garlic cloves from the strained mixture. Spoon off the fat from the juices and boil for 2–3 minutes to reduce and thicken a little.

Cut the chicken into serving portions, pour over a little of the juices and scatter with the garlic. Toast the baguette slices, then serve the chicken with the bread to be spread with the soft flesh squeezed from the garlic cloves.

Spicy roast chicken in banana leaves

Wrapping the chicken in banana leaves keeps the chicken moist and succulent while it cooks and creates a distinctive aroma and flavour.

Cooking time 1¾ hours
Serves 6

2 kg (4 lb 8 oz) chicken
3 tablespoons lemon juice
3–4 young banana leaves

Marinade
1 tablespoon oil
2 large onions, roughly chopped
4 garlic cloves, crushed
4 cm (1½ in) piece fresh ginger, roughly chopped
30 g (1 oz) ground almonds
½ teaspoon chilli powder
1 teaspoon ground turmeric
2 teaspoons garam masala
3 coriander (cilantro) roots, chopped
4 tablespoons chopped coriander (cilantro) leaves

Trim off any excess fat from the chicken. Pat it completely dry with paper towels and prick all over with a skewer so the marinade can penetrate the flesh. Rub the lemon juice and 1 teaspoon of salt all over the skin and inside the cavity of the chicken.

Heat the oil in a heavy-based frying pan over a low heat, add the onion and cook until the onion starts to brown. Add the garlic and ginger and cook for 2 minutes, or until soft. Add the almonds, chilli powder, turmeric and garam masala and cook for 1 minute. Allow the onion mixture to cool completely.

Put the cooled mixture and the coriander roots and leaves in a food processor or use a mortar and pestle to grind it to a smooth paste (you may need a little water). Rub the paste thoroughly all over the chicken and inside the cavity. Cover and refrigerate for 6 hours or overnight.

Preheat the oven to 200°C (400°F/Gas 6). Soften the banana leaves by dipping them into a pan of very hot water. Wipe the pieces dry as they become pliant. Tie the legs of the chicken together to keep them in place.

Wrap the chicken in the banana leaves, making sure that it is well covered. Tie a piece of kitchen string around the chicken like a parcel. If you can't buy banana leaves, wrap the chicken in a large sheet of foil instead. Put the chicken in a roasting tin and bake for 1½ hours. Unwrap the banana leaves or the foil from around the top of the chicken, baste the chicken with some of the juices and return it to the oven for 10 minutes, or until well browned. Check that the chicken is cooked by pulling away one leg — the juices should run clear. Rest the chicken for 10 minutes before carving.

Previous page: Roast chicken, Chicken with 40 cloves of garlic
Opposite: Spicy roast chicken in banana leaves

119

Chicken, mushroom and tarragon pie

A golden brown pastry encases tender, bite-sized pieces of chicken and an assortment of winter vegetables.

Cooking time 2½ hours
Serves 6

Pastry
290 g (1¼ cups) plain (all-purpose) flour
90 g (3¼ oz) butter, chilled and cubed
2 teaspoons finely chopped tarragon
2 tablespoons finely chopped flat-leaf (Italian) parsley
3–4 tablespoons iced water

Filling
500 ml (2 cups) chicken stock
750 g (1 lb 10 oz) chicken breast fillets
1 bay leaf
4 tablespoons butter
1 large leek, white part only, chopped
300 g (10½ oz) Swiss brown mushrooms
2 rashers bacon, chopped
1 small carrot, finely diced
1 celery stalk, finely diced
75 g (⅓ cup) plain (all-purpose) flour
125 ml (½ cup) crème fraîche
2 teaspoons Dijon mustard
3 garlic cloves, crushed
2 teaspoons finely chopped tarragon
115 g (½ cup) blanched fresh peas
1 egg
2 teaspoons milk

To make the pastry, sift the flour and a pinch of salt into a large bowl. Add the butter and rub it into the flour with your fingertips until the mixture resembles fine breadcrumbs. Stir in the chopped herbs. Make a well in the centre of the mixture, add almost all the water and mix with a flat–bladed knife using a cutting action until the mixture comes together in beads, adding a little more water if necessary. Gently gather the dough together and lift it out onto a lightly floured work surface. Press together into a ball, then flatten into a fat disc, wrap in plastic wrap and refrigerate for 30 minutes.

Bring the stock to a simmer in a saucepan, add the chicken breasts and bay leaf, cover and cook very gently for about 15 minutes or until the chicken is almost cooked through. Allow to cool in the cooking liquid. When cool enough to handle, lift out the chicken, straining and reserving the stock, and cut the chicken into bite-sized chunks.

Melt 1 tablespoon of butter in a saucepan and sauté the leek over a medium heat until soft but not coloured, then remove the leek and set aside. Put a little more butter in the pan, then add the mushrooms and a large pinch of salt and cook for 10 minutes or until all the liquid has evaporated. Set aside with the leek. Add the bacon and cook until just starting to brown, add to the mushrooms. Put a little more butter in the pan, add the carrots and celery and cook until starting to caramelize. Remove and add to the mushroom mixture. Melt another tablespoon of butter in the pan, add the flour and cook, stirring, for a minute, then gradually stir in 375 ml (1½ cups) of the warm stock until you have a smooth, fairly thick paste. Stir in the mustard, garlic, tarragon, peas and the reserved chicken and sautéed vegetable mixture. Stir in the crème fraîche and season. Allow to cool slightly then pour the mixture into a 2 litre (8 cup) round or oval ceramic baking dish.

Preheat the oven to 180°C (350°F/Gas 4). Roll out the pastry between two sheets of plastic wrap so that it is a little larger than the top of the pie dish. Put the pastry over the top of the dish and press the edges down firmly to seal. Trim any excess and make decorations if desired. Pierce a small air vent in the top of the pie with a sharp knife. Lightly beat the egg with the milk, then brush egg wash over the pastry. Put the pie in the oven and cook for 1 hour or until the pastry is golden. Rest for 15 minutes before serving.

Stuffed guinea fowl

In Tuscany, guinea fowl are often roasted; in Lombardy, they are sealed in clay and cooked in the oven; while in Veneto they are usually stuffed and cooked in an earthenware pot.

Cooking time 2 hours
Serves 4

100 g (3½ oz) dried borlotti beans or 400 g (14 oz) tinned
4 garlic cloves
1 bay leaf
4 tablespoons olive oil
25 g (1 oz) dried porcini
75 g (3 oz) green lentils
1 small onion, finely chopped
100 g (3½ oz) pancetta or smoked bacon, diced
100 g (3½ oz) almonds or pistachio nuts, chopped
1 sprig sage, chopped
1 x 1.5 kg (3 lb 5 oz) guinea fowl or 2 x 800 g (1 lb 12 oz) guinea
fowl, boned, leaving the wings and lower legs intact
2 tablespoons red wine

Soak the borlotti beans in cold water for at least 6 hours and then drain (if you are using tinned, you don't need to soak and precook). Put the beans in a saucepan of water, bring to the boil, then drain, rinsing away any foam. Return the beans to the saucepan, cover with water and bring to the boil, adding 2 garlic cloves, the bay leaf and a tablespoon of oil. Simmer gently for about 40 minutes, or until tender. Do not add salt to the beans or they will toughen. Drain and set aside.

Put the porcini in a bowl, cover with 150 ml (5 fl oz) hot water and leave to soak for 15 minutes. Cook the lentils in a saucepan of water with 1 garlic clove for about 20 minutes, or until the lentils are soft but not mushy. Drain well. Heat the remaining olive oil in a pan and cook the onion and pancetta until the onion is soft and the pancetta lightly browned.

Preheat the oven to 200°C (400°F/Gas 6). Spread the almonds or pistachios on a tray and roast for 10 minutes until light golden brown, then chop. Drain the porcini, reserving the soaking liquid, roughly chop them, then add to the onion mixture with the sage and the remaining garlic clove and stir to prevent browning. Stir in the drained beans, lentils and nuts. Cook for a few minutes and season to taste.

Push the stuffing into the cavity of the bird and sew up the opening with thick cotton or thin string. If you don't have any needles for this, seal the cavity with a couple of cocktail sticks. Tie the legs together. If you have any extra stuffing, cook it separately in a small covered dish for the last 20 minutes of cooking time. Brush the guinea fowl with oil.

Put the guinea fowl in an earthenware ovenproof dish and roast for 20 minutes, then reduce the heat to 180°C (350°F/Gas 4) and cook for 20 minutes more. Check the bird is cooked by piercing the thickest part of the thigh with a skewer (the juices should run clear) or gently pull away one of the legs from the body to test. Check the stuffing is cooked by pushing a skewer into the cavity for 3 seconds: the skewer should feel very hot when you pull it out. If it isn't, cover the bird with foil and cook until it is. Leave to rest for 15 minutes before serving, so the meat relaxes and becomes tender.

While the guinea fowl is resting, make a thin gravy by pouring the pan juices into a small saucepan. Add the liquid from the porcini and the red wine and simmer together. Season. Pour over the guinea fowl to serve.

Italian duck in red wine

In northern Italy duck is traditionally cooked with prosciutto or speck and a dry red wine.

Cooking time 3 hours
Serves 6–8

4 duck Marylands (leg quarters)
4 duck breasts
3 tablespoons butter
2 onions, finely chopped
2 carrots, cubed
2 celery stalks, cubed
120 g (4½ oz) prosciutto, in thin strips
750 ml (1 bottle) Barolo, or other dry red wine
2 bay leaves
4 tablespoons Cognac

Prick the duck pieces all over. Melt 2 tablespoons of butter in a large flameproof casserole dish or stockpot and fry the duck in batches over a medium heat, skin-side-down. When they have given up a good amount of fat and turned light golden brown, remove from the pot. Pour off all but 2 tablespoons of the fat.

Preheat the oven to 160°C (315°F/Gas 2–3). Add the onions, carrots, celery and prosciutto to the pot and cook over a low heat for about 8–10 minutes until golden. Add the duck and season with salt and freshly ground black pepper. Add 250 ml (1 cup) of wine, increase the heat and boil until the wine has reduced by half. Add the remaining wine and bay leaves and bring to the boil.

Cover the pot and transfer to the oven. Bake for 2 hours, or until tender. Transfer the duck pieces to a serving platter, cover with foil and keep warm. Put the pot over a high heat and bring to the boil. Add the remaining butter and Cognac and boil until thickened. Taste for seasoning. Spoon over the duck and serve at once.

Spanish duck with smoked paprika, pears and toasted almonds

This recipe echoes the cooking of Catalonia where nuts and fruit are often added to casseroles and stews. In this region of Spain, chocolate is also a common addition.

Cooking time 4½ hours
Serves 4

2 tablespoons oil
1 x 2 kg (4 lb 8 oz) duck, jointed into 8
1 small carrot, cut into chunks
1 onion, cut into chunks
2 bay leaves
1 sprig thyme
1 sprig parsley
6 peppercorns
¼ teaspoon freshly ground nutmeg
½ teaspoon sweet, smoked paprika
pinch ground cloves
60 g (2¼ oz) whole blanched almonds
8 shallots (scallions), peeled
8 baby carrots, trimmed
2 garlic cloves, peeled and cut into slivers
4 tablespoons rich cream sherry
1 cinnamon stick
4 firm ripe pears, halved and cored
25 g (1 oz) dark bittersweet chocolate, grated

Make the stock the day before using the wings and neck of the duck. Heat 1 tablespoon of oil in a large saucepan and, when hot, add the duck wings and neck and the chunks of carrot and onion. Brown over a medium heat for 15–20 minutes, stirring now and then.

Cover with 1.2 litres (5 cups) of cold water and add the bay leaves, thyme, parsley and peppercorns. Bring the liquid to the boil, then reduce to low. Cover and simmer very gently for 2 hours. Drain, discard the solids and leave to cool. Refrigerate overnight. The next day, lift off any fat that has set on the top of the stock. Preheat the oven to 180°C (350°F/Gas 4).

In a small bowl, mix the nutmeg, smoked paprika and cloves together with a little salt and pepper. Dust the raw duck pieces with the spice mixture. Heat the remaining oil in a flameproof casserole dish and, when hot, add half of the duck pieces. Brown well on both sides, then transfer to a large flameproof casserole dish. Repeat with the remaining duck.

Put the almonds on a baking tray and bake in the preheated oven for 5–7 minutes or until deeply golden. Set aside to cool.

Leaving a teaspoon of fat in the casserole, drain off the excess. Add the shallots and carrots to the dish and cook for 3–4 minutes or until lightly browned. Stir in the garlic and cook for a further 2 minutes. Pour in the sherry and bubble for a minute or so to deglaze the casserole. Pour in the stock and return the duck to the casserole with the cinnamon stick.

Bring to the boil. Cover and bake for 1 hour 10 minutes, turning halfway through. Put the pears on top of the duck and bake for a further 20 minutes. Meanwhile, tip the almonds into a food processor and blend until finely ground, then tip into a bowl. Add the chocolate and mix together.

When the duck is cooked, lift the pieces and the pears out of the liquid using a slotted spoon and transfer to a serving dish with the carrots, shallots and cinnamon stick. Keep warm.

Put the casserole over A direct heat and bring the liquid to the boil. Boil for 7–10 minutes or until the liquid has reduced its volume by half. Add 3 tablespoons of the hot liquid to the ground almonds and chocolate and stir to combine. Whisk the paste into the rest of the sauce to thicken. Season to taste, pour over the duck and serve.

Slow-cooked salted duck breasts

The combination of spices, herbs and salt that's rubbed over the duck makes for an aromatic and delicious meal.

Cooking time 1 hour 20 minutes
Serves 4

4 whole cloves
2 aniseed
2 teaspoons cracked black pepper
4 bay leaves
2 garlic cloves, chopped
115 g (½ cup) coarse butcher's salt (flossy fine grade — available from good butchers)
4 duck breasts
3 tablespoons pomegranate molasses
2 teaspoons olive oil

Preheat THE oven to 180°C (350°F/Gas 4). Roughly grind the cloves, aniseed, pepper and bay leaves with a mortar and pestle or coffee grinder. Add the spice and garlic to the salt and mix well. Put the salt mixture into a small roasting tray and bake in the preheated oven for 7–10 minutes or until fragrant. Reserve 3 tablespoons for the recipe and store any excess in a clean screw-top jar for future use.

Dry the duck breasts with a clean tea towel or kitchen paper and trim off any excess fat. Lightly sprinkle the breasts with the salt mixture, and put in a single layer in a ceramic or non-reactive container. Cover with plastic wrap and refrigerate for 18–24 hours.

Remove the duck breastS from the refrigerator and rinse well. Bring a large saucepan of water to a rapid boil over a high heat. When the water is boiling, add a duck breast, allow the water to return to the boil and blanch the breast for 1 minute. Remove the breast and wipe dry with a clean tea towel. Repeat with the remaining breasts and set aside to cool. Make sure the breasts are dry, then brush each one with pomegranate molasses, coating evenly. Set aside to dry. Lay the breasts in a single layer in a ceramic or non-reactive dish. Put them in the refrigerator, uncovered, to dry overnight.

Remove the breasts from the refrigerator half an hour before cooking to allow them to reach room temperature. Preheat the oven to 120°C (250°F/Gas ½). Heat the oil in a large frying pan over a moderate heat. Add two of the breasts, skin-side-down, to the hot pan and cook carefully for 4–5 minutes or until they reach an evenly deep brown colour. Repeat with the remaining breasts.

Put the duck, skin-side-up, into a large roasting tray, allowing some space between each breast, and cook in the preheated oven for 60 minutes. Remove from the heat, wrap with foil and allow to rest in a warm place for 10 minutes. Serve the duck sliced thinly.

Duckling with turnips

The white wine and stock in the roasting pan add flavour and help to keep the duck perfectly succulent and moist.

Cooking time 2 hours
Serves 2

1 x 1.8 kg (4 lb) duckling
bouquet garni
30 g (1 oz) clarified butter
1 carrot, chopped
1 celery stalk, chopped
½ large onion, chopped
2 teaspoons sugar
8 shallots (scallions)
8 baby turnips
100 ml (3½ fl oz) white wine
500 ml (2 cups) chicken stock
½ tablespoon softened butter
½ tablespoon plain (all-purpose) flour

Preheat the oven to 180°C (350°F/Gas 4) and put a roasting tin in the oven to heat up. Truss the duckling by tying the legs together and tying the wing tips together behind the body. Prick all over, put the bouquet garni in the cavity and season.

Heat the clarified butter in a large frying pan and brown the duckling on both sides. Lift the duckling out of the pan and pour all but a tablespoon of the fat into a jug. Add the carrot, celery and onion to the pan and soften over the heat, then brown. Remove the vegetables.

Add another 2 tablespoons of duck fat to the pan. Add the sugar and let it dissolve over a low heat. Turn up the heat and add the shallots and turnips. Caramelize over a high heat, then remove from the pan. Pour in the white wine and boil, stirring, for 30 seconds to deglaze the pan.

Put the carrot, celery and onion in the middle of the hot roasting tin, put the duckling on top and pour in the white wine and stock. Roast for 45 minutes. Baste well, add the turnips and shallots and roast for another 20 minutes. Baste again and roast for a further 25 minutes.

Lift out the duck, turnips and shallots and keep warm. Strain the sauce, pressing the chopped vegetables in the sieve to extract all the juices, then throw away the vegetables.

Pour the strained sauce into a saucepan and boil rapidly to reduce by half. Mix together the butter and flour, whisk into the sauce and boil, stirring, for 2 minutes until the mixture has thickened.

Put the duckling, turnips and shallots on a serving plate and pour a little sauce over them. Serve the rest of the sauce in a jug on the table.

Coulibiac

Coulibiac, or koulibiaca, is originally a Russian dish of flaked fish mixed with rice or semolina and encased in pastry.

Cooking time 50 minutes
Serves 6

60 g (2¼ oz) butter
1 onion, finely chopped
200 g (7 oz) button mushrooms, sliced
2 tablespoons lemon juice
220 g (8 oz) salmon fillet, boned, skinned, cut into pieces
2 hard-boiled eggs, chopped
2 tablespoons chopped dill
2 tablespoons chopped parsley
185 g (6½ oz) cooked rice, cooled
60 ml (¼ cup) thick (double/heavy) cream
1½ x 375 g (13 oz) blocks frozen puff pastry, thawed
1 egg, lightly beaten

Lightly grease a baking tray. Melt half the butter in a frying pan, then add the onion and cook over a medium heat for 5 minutes or until soft but not browned. Add the mushrooms and cook for 5 minutes. Add the lemon juice to the pan and stir to combine. Transfer the mixture to a bowl.

Melt the remaining butter in a pan, add the salmon and cook for 2 minutes. Transfer to a bowl, cool slightly and flake into large pieces. Add the egg, dill, parsley and salt and pepper. Gently combine and set aside.

Combine the rice and cream in a small bowl and season with salt and pepper.

Roll out the half block of pastry to a rectangle measuring 18 x 30 cm (9½ x 14 in) and put on the prepared baking tray. Spread half the rice mixture onto the pastry, leaving a 3 cm (1 in) border all the way around. Top with the salmon mixture, then the mushroom mixture, and finish with the remaining rice.

Roll out the full block of pastry to approximately 24 x 35 cm (8 x 12¼ in) and carefully put over the filling. Press the edges of the pastry together, then crimp to seal and decorate with pastry cut-outs. Refrigerate for 30 minutes.

Meanwhile, preheat the oven to 210°C (415°F/Gas 6–7). Brush the pastry with the lightly beaten egg and bake for 15 minutes. Reduce the heat to 180°C (350°F/Gas 4) and bake for another 15–20 minutes, or until the top is golden brown.

Baccalà alla gratinata

Start preparing the gratinata well in advance as you'll need to soak the salt out of the cod for a good 48 hours.

Cooking time 1 hour 50 minutes
Serves 6

600 g (1 lb 5 oz) baccalà (salt cod), cut into pieces about 15 cm (6 in) square
2 potatoes
60 ml (¼ cup) olive oil
375 ml (1½ cups) cream
1 sprig thyme
1 bay leaf
1 leek, finely chopped
6 garlic cloves, crushed
2 tablespoons finely chopped flat-leaf (Italian) parsley
a small squeeze of lemon juice
460 g (2 cups) fresh breadcrumbs
35 g (1¼ oz) butter, melted

Soak the cod in cold water in the fridge for 48 hours, changing the water every 8 hours. Simmer for 10 minutes, drain and simmer for another 10 minutes. Allow to cool slightly then remove all skin and bones and flake with a fork.

Preheat oven to 180°C (350°F/Gas 4). Boil the potatoes for 20 minutes or until tender. Drain well and, when the potatoes are cool enough to handle, peel them, then mash with a little olive oil. Meanwhile, put the cream, thyme and bay leaf in a small saucepan and bring to the boil. Remove from the heat and allow the flavours to infuse for 15 minutes, then strain, discarding the herbs.

Heat 1 tablespoon of the oil in a large saucepan and add the leek and 4 garlic cloves. Cook over a medium–low heat until starting to colour slightly, then quickly add the flaked cod and stir to combine. Beat in a little cream, then a little oil, and continue alternating until you have used up the oil — there should still be a little cream remaining. Add the potato and the remaining cream and beat the mixture until smooth. Remove from the heat, stir through half the parsley and season with salt, white pepper, lemon juice and remaining garlic.

Tip out into a lightly buttered 6-cup (1.5 litre) gratin dish and smooth over. Combine the breadcrumbs with the melted butter and remaining parsley, season well and sprinkle evenly over the top. Bake in the oven for 20–30 minutes or until the crumbs are golden. Serve with toasted baguette slices.

Note • This will keep for a couple of days in the fridge and can be served cold with toast, bread or crisp vegetables.

Baked trout with fennel and capers

You'll find the fennel and capers perfectly complement the trout, their flavour permeating the delicate flesh of the fish during baking.

Cooking time 1¾ hours
Serves 4

2 fennel bulbs, with fronds
1 leek, white part only, thickly sliced
1 large carrot, cut into batons
2 tablespoons olive oil
2 tablespoons capers, rinsed and patted dry
1 French shallot, finely chopped
4 x 300 g (10½ oz) brown or rainbow trout, gutted and fins removed
1 or 2 bay leaves, torn in half
25 g (1 oz) butter, cut into 4 cubes
4 slices lemon
200 ml (7 fl oz) fish stock
2 tablespoons dry vermouth
2 tablespoons thick (double/heavy) cream
2 tablespoons chopped chervil

Preheat the oven to 200°C (400°F/Gas 6). Cut off the fronds from the fennel bulbs and finely chop them. Thinly slice the bulbs and put in a roasting tin with the leek and carrot. Drizzle a tablespoon of olive oil over the vegetables, sprinkle with salt and pepper, then toss to coat them thoroughly. Bake on the middle shelf of the oven for 20 minutes.

Meanwhile, mix the chopped fennel fronds with the capers and shallot. Season the inside of the trout and fill with the fennel and caper stuffing. Put the bay leaves, cubes of butter and the lemon slices inside the fish too. Mix together the fish stock and vermouth.

Remove the vegetables from the oven, stir well and reduce the oven temperature to 140°C (275°F/Gas 1). Lay the trout over the vegetables and pour the stock and vermouth over the fish. Season the trout and drizzle with the remaining tablespoon of olive oil. Cover the top of the tin with foil and return to the oven for 1 hour 15 minutes or until the fish is cooked through. The flesh should feel flaky through the skin and the inside will look opaque and cooked. Lift the fish onto a large serving platter.

Transfer the tin of vegetables to the stovetop and heat for a couple of minutes, until the juices bubble and reduce. Now add the cream and cook for 1 minute, then stir in the chervil and season to taste. Spoon the vegetables around the fish on the platter, pour over a little of the juice and hand around the rest separately in a jug.

Baked polenta with four cheeses

If you have time, use 'proper' polenta instead of the instant variety. The constant stirring may seem labour intensive, but the flavour is much better.

Cooking time 1½ hours
Serves 6

Polenta
300 g (10½ oz) coarse-grain polenta
75 g (2½ oz) butter

Tomato sauce
3 tablespoons olive oil
2 garlic cloves, thinly sliced
1 tablespoon roughly chopped rosemary or thyme
800 g (1 lb 12 oz) tin chopped tomatoes

Cheese filling
200 g (7 oz) Gorgonzola cheese, cubed
250 g (9 oz) Taleggio cheese, cubed
250 g (9 oz) mascarpone cheese
100 g (3½ oz) Parmesan cheese, grated

Bring 1.5 litres (6 cups) of water to the boil in a heavy-based saucepan with 1 tablespoon salt. Add the polenta to the water in a gentle stream, whisking or stirring vigorously as you pour it in. Reduce the heat immediately so that the water is simmering. Stir continuously for the first 30 seconds to prevent any lumps appearing — the more you stir, the better the texture will be. Once you have stirred well at the beginning you can leave the polenta to mildly bubble away, stirring it every few minutes to prevent it sticking. Cook for 40 minutes. Add the butter and mix well.

Pour the polenta into a shallow casserole dish or baking tray about 5 cm (2 in) deep (you want the polenta to come no more than halfway up the side of the dish). Leave to cool completely.

To make the tomato sauce, heat the olive oil in a saucepan and cook the garlic gently until light brown. Add half the rosemary or thyme and then the tomatoes. Season with salt and pepper and cook gently, stirring occasionally, until reduced to a thick tomato sauce.

Preheat the oven to 180°C (350°F/Gas 4). Turn the polenta out of the dish and onto a board, then slice it horizontally in two. Pour half the tomato sauce into the bottom of the empty dish. Put the bottom slice of the polenta on top of the sauce and season. Scatter the Gorgonzola and Taleggio on top. Dot the mascarpone over the other cheeses with a teaspoon, and sprinkle with half the Parmesan and the remaining herbs.

Put the other layer of polenta on top and pour over the remaining tomato sauce. Sprinkle with the remaining Parmesan and bake for 30 minutes. Leave to rest for 10 minutes before serving with a simple salad.

Stuffed vegetables Provençal style

This wonderful dish from Provence makes good use of the region's abundance of fresh produce. You can use any herbs, meat or cheeses at hand.

Cooking time 1 hour 10 minutes
Serves 4

2 small eggplants (aubergines), halved lengthways
2 small zucchinis (courgettes), halved lengthways
4 tomatoes
2 small red capsicums (peppers), halved lengthways and seeded
4 tablespoons olive oil
2 red onions, chopped
2 garlic cloves, crushed
250 g (9 oz) minced (ground) pork
250 g (9 oz) minced (ground) veal
50 g (1¾ oz) tomato paste (purée)
80 ml (⅓ cup) white wine
2 tablespoons chopped parsley
50 g (1¾ oz) Parmesan cheese, grated
80 g (3 oz) fresh breadcrumbs
extra virgin olive oil

Preheat the oven to 180°C (350°F/Gas 4). Grease a large roasting tin with oil. Use a spoon to hollow out the centres of the eggplants and zucchinis, leaving a border around the edge. Chop the flesh finely.

Cut the tops from the tomatoes (don't throw away the tops). Use a spoon to hollow out the centres, catching the juice in a bowl, and chop the flesh roughly. Arrange the vegetables, including the capsicum, in the roasting tin. Brush the edges of the eggplant and zucchini with a little of the oil. Pour 125 ml (½ cup) of water into the roasting tin.

Heat half the oil in a large frying pan. Cook the onion and garlic for 3 minutes, or until they have softened. Add the minced pork and veal and stir for 5 minutes until the meat browns, breaking up any lumps with the back of a fork. Add the chopped eggplant and zucchini and cook for a further 3 minutes. Add the tomato pulp and juice, tomato paste and wine. Cook, stirring occasionally, for 10 minutes.

Remove the frying pan from the heat and stir in the parsley, Parmesan and breadcrumbs. Season well with salt and pepper. Spoon the mixture into the vegetables. Put the tops back on the tomatoes. Sprinkle the vegetables with the remaining olive oil and bake for 45 minutes, or until tender. Drizzle with extra virgin olive oil for serving.

Perfect sides

You don't want to let down a delectable main with a sad gathering of vegetables or a few pieces of wilted salad on the side. Here are some ideas that will bring a sense of occasion to any dinner, and which are also good enough to enjoy on their own.

Wet polenta

This polenta makes the perfect accompaniment to wet foods such as stews.

Cooking time 40 minutes
Serves 4

1 tablespoon salt
300 g (10½ oz) fine polenta
60 ml (¼ cup) olive oil
50 g (1¾ oz) butter
50 g (1¾ oz) Parmesan cheese, grated, plus extra to serve

Bring 1.5 litres (6 cups) of water to the boil in a deep heavy-based saucepan and add the salt. Add the polenta in a gentle stream, stirring vigorously as you pour. Reduce the heat immediately so the water is simmering and keep stirring for the first 30 seconds to prevent lumps appearing — the more you stir, the better the finished texture of the polenta. Leave the polenta to gently bubble away for about 40 minutes, stirring it every few minutes to stop it sticking to the pan. The finished polenta should drop from the spoon in thick lumps. Add the butter and Parmesan to the polenta and season with pepper. Sprinkle with extra Parmesan to serve.

Grilled polenta

For something a little different, serve grilled polenta with meat dishes instead of potatoes.

Cooking time 50 minutes
Serves 6

1 tablespoon salt
300 g (10½ oz) coarse-grain polenta
50 g (1¾ oz) butter
50 g (1¾ oz) Parmesan cheese, grated
olive oil, for brushing

Bring 1.5 litres (6 cups) of water to the boil in a deep heavy-based saucepan and add the salt. Add the polenta in a gentle stream, whisking or stirring vigorously as you pour. Reduce the heat immediately so the water is simmering and keep stirring for the first 30 seconds to prevent lumps appearing — the more you stir, the better the finished texture of the polenta. Leave the polenta to gently bubble away for about 40 minutes, stirring it every few minutes to stop it sticking to the pan. The finished polenta should drop from the spoon in thick lumps. Stir in the butter and Parmesan.

Pour the polenta onto a flat plate or serving dish and leave to cool at room temperature. Don't refrigerate, as this will create condensation and make the polenta stick when grilled. Preheat a griddle or grill (broiler). Cut the polenta into triangles or strips, brush with olive oil and grill for about 3 minutes on each side.

Couscous

Of course, you can steam the couscous with water, but stock will give it a much better flavour.

Cooking time 40 minutes
Serves 4

225 g (8 oz) medium-grain couscous
1 litre (4 cups) chicken stock

A couscoussier is a two–part steamer designed especially for cooking couscous. The top section has small perforations in the base and is very tight fitting. An ordinary steamer or a deep saucepan with a snugly–fitting colander will work well. To get a good seal, run a length of dampened muslin between the two sections, and spread a layer of muslin over the holes in the colander if they are particularly large.

Put the couscous in a sieve and rinse thoroughly under cold water. Turn out into a bowl and leave to swell for 5 minutes. Break up the lumps with a fork. Fill the bottom of the steamer with chicken stock (but not so full that it will touch the base of the section above when boiling), attach the top and bring to the boil.

Spread one–third of the couscous in the top and when steam rises through it, add the rest. Steam, uncovered, for 20 minutes. Turn it out onto a tray and spoon on 3–4 tablespoons of cold water. Sprinkle with salt and break up the lumps by gently lifting and turning the couscous over with oiled hands. Return to the steamer and continue steaming for another 20 minutes. Turn out onto a serving plate. Pour on a couple of tablespoons of the hot stock and work it through, breaking up the lumps. Cover with foil and leave to swell for 10 minutes before serving.

Milanese risotto

Milanese risotto, the classic accompaniment to osso buco, takes its brilliant yellow colour from saffron and its rich flavour from beef marrow.

Cooking time 40 minutes
Serves 6

200 ml (7 fl oz) dry white vermouth or white wine
large pinch saffron threads
1½ litres (6 cups) chicken stock
100 g (3½ oz) butter
75 g (2½ oz) beef marrow
1 large onion, finely chopped
1 garlic clove, crushed
350 g (12 oz) risotto rice
50 g (1¾ oz) Parmesan cheese, grated

Put the vermouth in a bowl, add the saffron and leave to soak. Put the stock in a saucepan, bring to the boil and then maintain at a low simmer.

Melt the butter and marrow in a large, wide, heavy-based saucepan. Add the onion and garlic and cook until softened but not browned. Add the rice and reduce the heat to low. Season and stir briefly to thoroughly coat the rice.

Add the vermouth and saffron to the rice. Increase the heat and cook, stirring, until all the liquid has been absorbed. Stir in a ladleful of the simmering stock and cook over a moderate heat, stirring continuously. When the stock has been absorbed, stir in another ladleful. Continue like this for about 20 minutes, until all the stock has been added and the rice is cooked. (You may not need to use all the stock, or you may need a little extra — every risotto will be slightly different.)

Stir in a handful of Parmesan and serve the rest on the side for people to help themselves.

Tian de legumes

The term 'tian' refers to both the shallow dish used for baking gratins and the dishes that are cooked in it.

Cooking time 3 hours
Serves 6–8

500 g (1 lb 2 oz) sweet potato (kumera)
1¼ kg (2 lb 12 oz) potatoes
4 large leeks
3 garlic cloves
¾ teaspoon nutmeg
3 bay leaves
300 ml (10½ fl oz) cream

Preheat the oven to 170°C (325°F/Gas 3) and grease a 26 x 28 x 7 cm (10 x 11 x 3 in) tian or shallow, ovenproof ceramic dish. Peel and thinly slice the sweet potato and potatoes. Slice the leeks into rings. Thinly slice the garlic.

Layer half the potatoes in the bottom of the prepared dish. Scatter a few slices of garlic over them and toss in a bay leaf. Sprinkle lightly with salt and pepper, and ¼ teaspoon of the nutmeg. Scatter the leeks over the top, some garlic slices and a bay leaf, and sprinkle with salt and pepper and ¼ teaspoon of nutmeg. Layer the sweet potato, some garlic slices and a bay leaf and season as above with salt, pepper and nutmeg. Finally, make a layer with the last of the potatoes and season lightly. Pour the cream over the top.

Cover with foil and bake for 2½–3 hours, or until the vegetables are very tender. After 2 hours, remove the foil to allow the top to become crisp and golden. Remove from the oven and rest for 5 minutes before serving.

White bean purée

As well as being a side dish, white bean purée is delicious as a dip or spread on crusty bread.

Cooking time 5 minutes
Serves 4

2 x 400 g (14 oz) tins cannellini beans, drained and rinsed
95 g (½ cup) ground almonds
1 tablespoon lemon juice
3 cloves garlic, chopped
125 ml (½ cup) olive oil
1 teaspoon finely chopped oregano

Put the beans, almonds, lemon juice and garlic in a food processor and process until the mixture is smooth. While the motor is running, gradually add the oil and process until thick and creamy.

Transfer to a saucepan over low heat and stir until heated through. Season, and stir through the oregano.

Sautéed spinach

This spinach perfectly complements the flavours of beef or lamb dishes.

Cooking time 5 minutes
Serves 4

1 kg (2 lb 4 oz) English spinach
2 tablespoons olive oil
1 garlic clove

Wash the spinach thoroughly and shake it dry, leaving just a little water clinging to the leaves. Put into a deep saucepan in batches and cook, covered, until just wilted. Wipe the saucepan dry and add the oil. Add the garlic and cook for a few seconds, then add the spinach. Cover the pan for a minute to create some steam. Remove the lid and turn up the heat, stirring the spinach until all the liquid has evaporated. Season with salt and pepper before serving.

Spiced cabbage

A favourite vegetable dish from Northern India that's usually served with other mains, and breads such as parathas or chapatis. It's an excellent side for chicken curry.

Cooking time 20 minutes
Serves 4

½ onion, roughly chopped
1 garlic clove, roughly chopped
2.5 cm (1 in) piece fresh ginger, chopped
2 green chillies, deseeded and chopped
4 tablespoons oil
1 teaspoon cumin seeds
1 teaspoon ground turmeric
500 g (1 lb 2 oz) green cabbage, finely shredded
1 teaspoon salt
½ teaspoon ground black pepper
2 teaspoons ground cumin
1 teaspoon ground coriander
¼ teaspoon chilli powder
20 g (1 oz) unsalted butter

Put the onion, garlic, ginger and chilli in a food processor and whiz until finely chopped but not blended to a paste, or chop together with a knife.

Heat the oil in a heavy-based frying pan over a low heat and fry the onion mixture until softened but not browned. Add the cumin seeds and turmeric to the pan and stir for 1 minute. Mix in the cabbage, stirring thoroughly until all the leaves are coated in the yellow paste. Add the salt, pepper, ground cumin, coriander and chilli powder. Stir to coat the cabbage, then cook for 10 minutes with the pan partially covered, stirring occasionally until the cabbage is soft. If the cabbage becomes too dry and starts sticking to the pan, add 1–2 tablespoons water. Stir in the butter and season with salt.

Chinese broccoli in oyster sauce

Chinese broccoli has long stems, tiny florets and a slightly bitter flavour. It's available from Chinese grocery stores.

Cooking time 10 minutes
Serves 6

1 kg (2 lb 4 oz) Chinese broccoli (gai lan)
1½ tablespoons oil
2 spring onions (scallions), finely chopped
1½ tablespoons grated fresh ginger
3 garlic cloves, finely chopped
3 tablespoons oyster sauce
1½ tablespoons light soy sauce
1 tablespoon Shaoxing rice wine
1 teaspoon sugar
1 teaspoon roasted sesame oil
125 ml (½ cup) chicken stock
2 teaspoons cornflour

Wash the broccoli well and discard any tough-looking stems. Cut diagonally into small pieces through the stem and the leaf. Blanch the broccoli in a saucepan full of boiling water for 2 minutes, or until the stems and leaves are just tender, then refresh in cold water and dry thoroughly.

Heat a wok over a high heat, add the oil and heat until very hot. Stir-fry the spring onion, ginger and garlic for about 10 seconds, or until fragrant. Add the broccoli and cook until the broccoli is heated through. Combine the remaining ingredients, add to the wok, stirring until the sauce has thickened, and toss to coat the broccoli.

Slow-roasted balsamic tomatoes

The flavour of ripe tomatoes is intensified as they roast slowly. Serve with grilled fish and meats or on an antipasto platter.

Cooking time 2½ hours
Makes 40

10 firm, ripe Roma (plum) tomatoes
8 garlic cloves, crushed
4 tablespoons caster (superfine) sugar
4 tablespoons torn basil leaves
4 teaspoons chopped oregano leaves
few drops good-quality balsamic vinegar

Preheat the oven to 140°C (275°F/Gas 1). Line two baking trays with baking paper. Slice each tomato lengthways into quarters and put the quarters in rows on the trays.

Mix the garlic with the sugar, basil, oregano and balsamic vinegar. Using clean fingers, put a little of the mixture onto the sides of each tomato quarter and season with salt and pepper.

Bake in the oven for 2½ hours. The tomatoes are ready when they are slightly shrivelled at the edge and semi-dried (they should still be soft in the middle). Eat warm or cold and store in the refrigerator.

Pommes Anna

There are very few mains that can't be improved with a side of potatoes in any of their myriad forms.

Cooking time 1 hour
Serves 4

850 g (1 lb 14 oz) waxy potatoes
125 g (4½ oz) butter, melted

Preheat the oven to 210°C (415°F/Gas 6–7). Grease a 20 cm (8 in) round cake tin or ovenproof dish with melted butter.

Peel the potatoes and cut into very thin slices with a mandolin or sharp knife. Lay the potato slices on paper towels and pat dry. Starting from the centre of the dish, overlap one-fifth of the potato slices over the base. Drizzle one-fifth of the butter over the top. Season well.

Repeat the layers four more times, drizzling the last bit of butter over the top. Cut a circle of greaseproof paper to fit over the top of the potato. Bake for about 1 hour, or until cooked and golden and a knife blade slides easily into the centre. Remove from the oven and leave for 5 minutes, then pour off any excess butter. Run a knife around the edge to loosen, then turn out onto a serving plate.

Mashed potato

An all-time favourite eaten with steaks, stews, sausages and just about any meat that needs a bit on the side.

Cooking time 12 minutes
Serves 4

1 kg (2 lb 4 oz) floury potatoes
200 ml (7 fl oz) milk
4 tablespoons butter
freshly grated nutmeg
butter, for serving

Cut the potatoes into large even pieces and cook them in boiling salted water for 12 minutes, or until they are tender to the point of a knife.

Drain well. Put the milk in the saucepan with the butter and heat briefly. Add the potatoes and mash until very smooth. Season with salt, pepper and nutmeg. Serve with extra butter.

Previous page: Chinese broccoli in oyster sauce, Slow-roasted balsamic tomatoes
Opposite: Pommes Anna

Celeriac mash

Take an ordinary mash and make it into something a little special.

Cooking time 15 minutes
Serves 4

1 celeriac
1 potato, cubed
250 ml (1 cup) milk
1 tablespoon butter

Peel and chop the celeriac. Put the pieces into a bowl of water as you cut them or they will turn brown if exposed to the air. Put the potato and celeriac in a saucepan with the milk and bring to the boil.

Cover and cook for 15 minutes until the celeriac and potato are tender and then mash them together with the milk they were cooked in. Season well and incorporate the butter.

Potato gnocchi

Serve with a basic tomato, or an oil and garlic, sauce and sprinkle with grated Parmesan cheese.

Cooking time 1 hour 5 minutes
Serves 4

1 kg (2 lb 4 oz) floury potatoes, unpeeled
2 egg yolks
2 tablespoons grated Parmesan cheese
125–185 g (4½–6½ oz) plain (all-purpose) flour

Preheat the oven to 180°C (350°F/Gas 4). Prick the potatoes all over and bake for 1 hour, or until tender. Cool for 15 minutes, then peel and mash (do not use a food processor or the potatoes will become gluey).

Mix in the yolks and Parmesan, then gradually stir in the flour. When the mixture gets too dry for you to use a spoon, use your hands. Once a loose dough forms, transfer it to a lightly floured surface and knead gently. Work in enough extra flour to give a very soft, light, pliable dough.

Divide the dough into six portions. Dust your hands lightly in flour, then, working with one portion at a time, roll out on a floured surface to make a rope about 1.5 cm (¾ in) thick. Cut into 1.5 cm (¾ in) lengths. Take each piece of dough and press your finger into it to form a concave shape, then roll the outer surface over the tines of a fork to make deep ridges. Fold the outer lips in towards each other to make a hollow in the middle. Put on a lightly floured tray and leave to rest for 10 minutes.

Bring a large saucepan of salted water to the boil, then reduce the heat a little. Add the gnocchi in batches, stir gently and return to the boil. Cook until they rise to the surface. Remove with a slotted spoon and drain.

Potato and leek al forno

An Italian dish that goes particularly well with roast meats and stews.

Cooking time 1¼ hours
Serves 4

3 tablespoons butter
400 g (14 oz) leeks, trimmed, halved and sliced
3 garlic cloves, thinly sliced
1 tablespoon chopped thyme
1 kg (2 lb 4 oz) potatoes
350 g (12 oz) mascarpone cheese
250 ml (1 cup) vegetable stock

Thinly slice the potatoes with a mandolin or very sharp knife (they must be thin or they will not cook through evenly). Preheat the oven to 180°C (350°F/Gas 4). Heat the butter or oil in a saucepan and cook the leeks over a low heat for about 10 minutes, or until soft. Season with salt and pepper. Add the garlic and herbs and cook for a couple of minutes.

Grease a shallow, 3-litre (12-cup) capacity gratin dish with butter or oil. Arrange a layer of potatoes in the base of the dish and season with salt and pepper. Scatter with one-third of the leeks and a few dollops of mascarpone. Continue in the same way to make two more layers, finishing with a layer of potatoes, then top with mascarpone. Pour the stock over the top and cover with foil. Bake in the oven for about 1 hour, removing the foil for the last 15 minutes to brown the top.

Boulangère potatoes

Here's another good reason why you should always have some home-made stock in the freezer.

Cooking time 1 hour
Serves 6

1 kg (2 lb 4 oz) potatoes
1 large onion
2 tablespoons finely chopped parsley
500 ml (2 cups) hot chicken or vegetable stock
25 g (1 oz) butter, cubed

Preheat the oven to 180°C (350°F/Gas 4).

Thinly slice the potatoes and onion with a mandolin or sharp knife. Build up alternate layers of potato and onion in a 20 x 10 cm (8 x 4 in) deep ovenproof dish, sprinkling parsley, salt and black pepper between each layer. Finish with a layer of potato. Pour the stock over the top and dot with butter.

Bake, covered with foil, on the middle shelf of the oven for 30 minutes, then remove the foil and lightly press down on the potatoes to keep them submerged in the stock. Bake for another 30 minutes, or until the potatoes are tender and the top golden brown. Serve piping hot.

Previous page: Mashed potato and Celeriac mash, Potato and leek al forno and Boulangère potatoes
Opposite: Potato gnocchi

A happy ending

No dinner is complete without a little taste of something sweet. So add the finishing touch to your party with a dessert designed to tantalize the tastebuds, and send your guests home with the contented feeling that the world is quite as it should be.

Chocolate and almond torte

This superb combination of chocolate and almonds is perfected with a dollop of crème fraîche.

Cooking time 1¼ hours
Serves 8–10

150 g (5½ oz) flaked or whole almonds
1 slice pandoro or 1 small brioche
300 g (10½ oz) dark chocolate
2 tablespoons brandy
150 g (5½ oz) unsalted butter, softened
150 g (5½ oz) caster (superfine) sugar
4 eggs
1 teaspoon vanilla extract (optional)
200 g (7 oz) mascarpone cheese
crème fraîche
cocoa

Preheat the oven to 170°C (325°F/Gas 4). Toast the almonds in the oven for 3–4 minutes until golden brown.

Put the almonds and pandoro in a food processor and process until the mixture resembles coarse breadcrumbs. Alternatively, finely chop the nuts and pandoro and mix them together. Grease a 23 cm (10 in) springform tin with a little butter. Tip some of the mixture into the tin and shake it around so that it forms a coating on the bottom and side of the tin. Put the remaining nut mixture aside.

Gently melt the chocolate and brandy in a heatproof bowl set over a saucepan of simmering water. Make sure that the bowl does not touch the water and that the water does not get into the bowl or the chocolate will seize. You can also melt the chocolate in a microwave. Stir occasionally until the chocolate has melted. Cool slightly.

Cream the butter and sugar in the food processor or with a wooden spoon for a few minutes until light and pale. Add the melted chocolate, eggs, vanilla and mascarpone. Add the remaining nut mixture and mix well. Tip into the tin. Bake for 50–60 minutes or until just set. Leave to rest in the tin for about 15 minutes before taking out. When cool, dust with a little cocoa powder, if desired. Serve with crème fraîche sprinkled with a little more cocoa, if you like.

Chocolate pots with hazelnut toffee

The superb silken texture of this dessert is only achieved after several hours' refrigeration — if you can last that long. If not, it is also delicious served warm.

Cooking time 1½ hours
Serves 8

250 g (9 oz) good-quality dark chocolate
580 ml (2⅓ cups) cream
6 large egg yolks
80 g (⅓ cup) caster (superfine) sugar
1 tablespoon freshly brewed espresso coffee
2 tablespoons Frangelico or other hazelnut liqueur
80 g (⅔ cup) whole hazelnuts
230 g (1 cup) caster (superfine) sugar

Preheat the oven to 150°C (300°F/Gas 2). Finely chop the chocolate and put in a heatproof bowl.

Gently heat the cream in a small saucepan over a medium heat. Bring it just to a simmer (don't allow to boil), then quickly remove it from the heat and pour over the chocolate. Stir constantly until the chocolate has completely melted — this will take about 5 minutes. The mixture should be smooth and have an even colour.

Whisk the egg yolks with the sugar just to combine, then gradually stir in the chocolate mixture, then the coffee and liqueur. Strain the mixture through a fine sieve. Allow to settle and cool slightly, then skim off any foam on the surface.

Divide the mixture between 8 x 125 ml (½ cup) ramekins or dariole moulds, filling to just below the top. Check for any air bubbles on top and gently prick with a fine skewer or tap lightly on the bench.

Cover each ramekin tightly with foil. Put them into a large baking dish, ensuring they are evenly spaced and not too close to the edge of the dish, then pour in enough hot water to reach about halfway up the sides of the ramekins. Cook for 1 hour, then check them by gently shaking a ramekin — the mixture should be set but still wobble a little in the middle.

Take the ramekins out of the Pan, remove the foil and allow them to cool completely before covering and refrigerating for at least 3 hours or until well chilled. Serve the chocolate pots accompanied by the hazelnut toffee.

To make the toffee, toast the hazelnuts until aromatic, then spread them out on a lightly buttered baking tray while you make the caramel. Put the sugar and 250 ml (1 cup) water in a small pan over a high heat and stir until the sugar has dissolved. Bring to the boil, then turn down the heat and simmer for 8 minutes or until the toffee has turned a deep amber, swirling the pan occasionally so that it cooks evenly. Take off the heat immediately and pour the toffee over the hazelnuts on the tray. Put aside and allow to set. When cool, break into uneven pieces.

New York cheesecake

You don't have to be in the city that never sleeps to get a taste for life in the fast lane. Serve with a good, strong brew of coffee.

Cooking time 1 hour 50 minutes
Serves 8–10

Pastry
115 g (½ cup) self-raising flour
230 g (1 cup) plain (all-purpose) flour
60 g (¼ cup) caster (superfine) sugar
1 teaspoon grated lemon zest
80 g (3 oz) butter
1 egg

Filling
750 g (1 lb 10 oz) curd or cream cheese, softened
230 g (1 cup) caster (superfine) sugar
60 g (¼ cup) plain (all-purpose) flour
2 teaspoons grated orange zest
2 teaspoons grated lemon zest
4 eggs
170 ml (⅔ cup) cream

glacé citrus slices

Process the flours, sugar, lemon zest and butter for 30 seconds, until crumbly. Add the egg and process until the mixture just comes together. Knead on a floured surface, wrap in plastic wrap and refrigerate for 20 minutes, or until firm.

Preheat the oven to 210°C (410°F/Gas 6–7). Roll the pastry between two sheets of baking paper until large enough to fit the base and sides of a greased 22 cm (8 in) round springform cake tin. Ease into the tin and trim the edges. Bake blind for 10 minutes, remove the baking paper and beans, flatten the pastry lightly with the back of a spoon and bake for 5 minutes. Cool.

To make the filling, reduce the oven to 150°C (300°F/Gas 2). Beat the cream cheese, sugar, flour and zest until smooth. Add the eggs, one at a time, beating after each addition. Beat in the cream, pour the filling over the pastry and bake for 1 hour 25 minutes or until almost set. Cool, then refrigerate. Dust with icing sugar before serving. Serve with glacé citrus slices if you like.

Bread and butter pudding

For something a little different, you can use fruit loaf or brioche to give an old favourite a new taste.

Cooking time 1–1¼ hours
Serves 6

90 g (3¼ oz) sultanas
3 tablespoons brandy
12 slices good-quality white bread or brioche, crusts removed
60 g (2¼ oz) unsalted butter, softened
3 tablespoons marmalade
3 eggs
3 egg yolks
200 g (7 oz) caster (superfine) sugar
1 teaspoon natural vanilla extract
750 ml (3 cups) milk
375 ml (1½ cups) cream
3 tablespoons demerara sugar

Soak the sultanas in the brandy for 30 minutes or until slightly plump. Lightly grease a 10-cup (2.5 litre) capacity shallow, ovenproof dish. Butter the slices of bread, brush with marmalade and cut into diagonal quarters. Arrange the bread in two layers, butter-side-up in the dish. Drain the sultanas and scatter between the layers of bread. Reserve any remaining brandy.

Whisk together the eggs and yolks, sugar, vanilla and any reserved brandy. Whisk in the milk and cream and pour over the bread. Leave in the refrigerator to soak for 1 hour.

Preheat the oven to 160°C (315°F/Gas 2–3). Remove the pudding from the refrigerator and sprinkle with the demerara sugar. Put the dish in a roasting tin three-quarters full of hot water and bake in the preheated oven for 1–1¼ hours or until the custard is set and the bread slightly puffed and golden on top.

Sticky golden sponge pudding

Delicious served warm with homemade custard or a generous scoop of vanilla ice cream, this is one pudding that rarely lasts long on the plate.

Cooking time 2 hours
Serves 4

120 g (4 oz) unsalted butter, softened
120 g (4 oz) caster (superfine) sugar
1 teaspoon natural vanilla extract
2 eggs
120 g (4 oz) self-raising flour, sifted
2 tablespoons milk
½ cup (125 fl oz) golden syrup

Lightly grease a 1-litre (4-cup capacity) pudding basin. Put the empty basin in a large saucepan on a trivet or upturned saucer and pour enough cold water into the saucepan to come halfway up the side of the basin. Remove the basin and put the water on to boil.

Cream the butter and sugar in a small bowl until light and fluffy. Add the vanilla. Gradually add the eggs, beating well after each addition and alternating with a little flour.

Use a large metal spoon or rubber spatula to gently fold in the sifted flour. Add the milk and gently stir to combine. Pour the golden syrup into the base of the pudding basin and spoon over the sponge mixture.

Lay a sheet of foil on the work surface and cover with a sheet of baking paper. Make a large pleat in the middle. Grease the paper and put, paper-side-down, across the top of the basin and tie string securely around the rim of the basin and over the top to make a handle. The string handle is used to lift the pudding out of the pan.

Gently lower the basin into the boiling water, reduce to a fast simmer and cover with a tight-fitting lid. Cook for 2 hours, checking the water every half an hour and topping up to the original level with boiling water as needed.

Remove from the saucepan, test with a skewer or by pressing the top gently — it should be firm in the centre and well risen. If not cooked, re-cover and cook until done. Turn the pudding out onto a dish. If desired, you can serve a jug of warmed golden syrup separately. Serve with custard or cream.

Tres-leches (three-milk) cake

A delicious labour of love, this cake must be bathed repeatedly in milk and cream. This can't be rushed, as the sponge needs time to soak up the mixture for a rich, moist finish.

Cooking time 1 hour
Serves 12

6 eggs
230 g (1 cup) caster (superfine) sugar
125 ml (½ cup) milk
2½ teaspoons natural vanilla extract
290 g (1¼ cups) plain (all-purpose) flour
2 teaspoons baking powder
½ teaspoon cream of tartar
395 g (14 oz) tin condensed milk
375 g (13 oz) tin evaporated milk
300 ml (10½ fl oz) cream
2½ tablespoons white rum

Meringue topping
290 g (1¼ cups) caster (superfine) sugar
4 egg whites
½ teaspoon cream of tartar

Preheat your oven to 170°C (325°F/Gas 3). Grease a 22 cm (9 in) square deep cake tin and line the bottom with baking paper. Separate the eggs then beat the yolks with all but 2 tablespoons of the sugar until pale, thick and creamy. Fold in the milk, 1 teaspoon of vanilla extract, sifted flour and baking powder and mix until well combined. Whisk the egg whites until frothy, add the cream of tartar and continue to whisk until they form soft peaks. Gradually whisk in the reserved sugar and continue to whisk until you have firm, glossy peaks, but don't allow them to become stiff and dry.

Beat a spoonful of the whites into the cake mix then gently fold in the rest until well combined. Pour into the cake tin and cook on the middle rack of the oven for about 45–50 minutes or until a cake skewer comes out clean. The top should be a deep golden brown. Cool completely on a wire cake rack before inverting onto a large platter with a decent lip to catch the overflow from the milk mixture. Using a fine skewer, prick deep holes all over the cake.

Combine the condensed and evaporated milks with the cream, and the remaining 1½ teaspoons of vanilla and rum, then pour a small amount over the top of the cake and allow it to be soaked up. Continue to do this until all the mixture is soaked up. Spoon the overflow back over the cake as it accumulates in the serving dish. The soaking can take up to an hour and the absorption rate will slow down as the cake becomes fuller.

To make the meringue, put the sugar with 80 ml (⅓ cup) water in a small saucepan over a high heat and stir until the sugar has dissolved. Allow the syrup to boil without stirring for about 8 minutes or until it reaches softball stage. To test if it is ready, drop a little of the sugar mixture from a spoon into a small bowl of cold water — it should form a small soft lump.

Meanwhile, whisk the egg whites until frothy, then add the cream of tartar and whisk until soft peaks form. Slowly add the boiling syrup in a thin stream. Continue to whisk until the mixture is very thick and cool to touch. The heat from the sugar will cook the egg white, forming a soft meringue.

Spread the meringue over the top and sides of the cake with a spatula dipped in hot water. Refrigerate the cake, uncovered, for at least 3 hours to allow the milk mixture to settle throughout the cake and develop the flavours.

Serve the cake on its own or accompanied by some fresh berries, mango or banana or some lightly poached stone fruits.

Apple crumble

You can make crumble with just about any kind of fruit but, if you choose soft fruit such as strawberries or raspberries, remember that they will break down as they cook.

Cooking time 1 hour
Serves 6

8 Golden Delicious apples
4 tablespoons caster (superfine) sugar
zest of 1 lemon
120 g (4½ oz) butter
120 g (4½ oz) plain (all-purpose) flour
1 teaspoon ground cinnamon

Turn the oven to 180°C (350°/Gas 4). Peel and core the apples, then cut them into chunks. Put the apple, 2 tablespoons of sugar and the lemon zest in a small baking dish and mix together. Dot 40 g (about 2 tablespoons) of butter over the top.

Rub the remaining butter into the flour until you have a texture which resembles coarse sand. Stir through the rest of the sugar and the cinnamon.

Sprinkle the crumble mixture over the apple and bake the crumble for 1 hour, by which time the top should be browned and the juice bubbling up through the crumble. Serve with thick cream or custard.

Tarte Tatin

There are few things as tempting as a sweet, caramelly apple tart
served with lashings of cream on the side — the richer the better.

Cooking time 1 hour 10 minutes
Serves 8

225 g (8 oz) plain (all-purpose) flour
small pinch salt
100 g (3½ oz) unsalted butter
65 g (2½ oz) icing (confectioners') sugar
1 large egg, beaten
1.5 kg (3 lb 5 oz) dessert apples
70 g (2½ oz) unsalted butter
185 g (6½ oz) caster (superfine) sugar

Sift the flour and salt onto a work surface and make a well in the
centre. Put the butter into the well and, using a pecking action with
your fingertips and thumb, work it until it is very soft. Add the sugar
to the butter and mix together. Add the egg to the butter and mix
together.

Gradually incorporate the flour, flicking it onto the mixture and then
chopping through it until you have a rough dough. Bring together
with your hands and then knead a few times to make a smooth
dough. Roll into a ball, wrap in plastic wrap and put in the fridge for
at least 1 hour.

Peel, core and cut the apples into quarters. Put the butter and sugar
in a deep 25 cm (10 in) frying pan with an ovenproof handle. Heat
until the butter and sugar have melted together. Arrange the apples
tightly, one by one, in the frying pan, making sure there are no gaps.
Remember that you will be turning the tart out the other way up, so
arrange the apple pieces so that they are neat underneath.

Cook over a low heat for 35–40 minutes, or until the apple is soft,
the caramel lightly browned and any excess liquid has evaporated.
Baste the apple with a pastry brush every so often, so that the top is
caramelized as well. Preheat the oven to 190°C (375°F/Gas 5).

Roll out the pastry on a lightly floured surface into a circle slightly
larger than the frying pan. Lay the pastry over the apple and press
down around the edge to enclose it completely. Roughly trim the
edge of the pastry and then fold the edge back on itself to give a
neat finish.

Bake for 25–30 minutes, or until the pastry is golden and cooked.
Remove from the oven and leave to rest for 5 minutes before turning
out. (If any apple sticks to the pan, just push it back into the hole in
the tart.) Serve with a dollop of thick (double/heavy) cream.

Pear and almond tart

An irresistible combination of fruit and nuts encased in mouthwatering pastry.

Cooking time 1 hour 10 minutes
Serves 8

Pastry
350 g (12 oz) plain (all-purpose) flour
small pinch salt
150 g (5½ oz) unsalted butter
100 g (3½ oz) icing (confectioners') sugar
2 eggs, beaten

Pear filling
50 g (1¾ oz) caster (superfine) sugar
1 vanilla pod
3 pears (ripe but still firm), peeled, halved and cored

Almond filling
150 g (5½ oz) unsalted butter, softened
150 g (5½ oz) caster (superfine) sugar
few drops natural vanilla extract
2 large eggs, lightly beaten
140 g (5 oz) ground almonds
finely grated zest of 1 small lemon
25 g (1 oz) plain (all-purpose) flour

3 tablespoons apricot jam

To make the pastry, sift the flour and salt onto a work surface and make a well in the centre. Put the butter into the well and, using a pecking action with your fingertips and thumb, work it until it is very soft. Add the icing sugar to the butter and mix. Add the eggs to the butter and mix well.

Gradually incorporate the flour, flicking it onto the mixture and then chopping through it until you have a rough dough. Bring together with your hands and then knead a few times to make a smooth dough. Roll into a ball, wrap in plastic wrap and put in the fridge for at least 1 hour.

To make the almond filling, beat the butter, sugar and vanilla extract together until pale and creamy. Beat in the eggs gradually and then fold in the almonds, lemon zest and flour.

Preheat the oven to 190°C (375°F/Gas 5). Roll out the pastry to line a 23 x 2.5 cm (9 x 1 in) round loose-based fluted tart tin. Chill in the fridge for 20 minutes.

Put the sugar and vanilla pod in a saucepan. Add the pears and pour in just enough water to cover them, then remove the pears. Bring the water to a simmer and cook for 5 minutes. Add the pears, cover and poach for 5–10 minutes until tender. Drain and leave to cool.

Line the pastry shell with a crumpled piece of greaseproof paper and baking beads (use dried beans or rice if you don't have beads). Blind bake the pastry for 10 minutes, remove the paper and beads and bake for a further 3–5 minutes, or until the pastry is just cooked but still very pale. Reduce the oven temperature to 180°C (350°F/Gas 4).

Spread three-quarters of the filling in the pastry shell and put the pear halves on top, cut-side-down and stalk ends in the middle. Fill the gaps with the remaining filling. Bake for 35–40 minutes, or until the filling is golden and firm. Melt the jam with 1 teaspoon water, sieve out any lumps and brush over the pears to make them shine.

Kulfi

Kulfi are an Indian treat worth making at home.

Cooking time 2 hours
Makes 12

2 litres (8 cups) milk
10 cardamom pods, lightly crushed
6 tablespoons sugar
15 g (½ oz) almonds, blanched and finely chopped
15 g (½ oz) pistachio kernels, finely chopped

Put the milk and cardamom pods in a heavy-based saucepan and bring to the boil. Reduce the heat to low and simmer, stirring frequently, for about 2 hours, until the milk has reduced to one-third of the original amount, about 750 ml (3 cups). Whenever a thin skin forms on top, stir it back in.

Add the sugar to the pan, simmer for 5 minutes, then strain into a shallow plastic freezer box. Add the almonds and half the pistachio kernels, then cool. Put 12 x 75 ml (⅓-cup capacity) kulfi or dariole moulds in the freezer to chill.

Put the kulfi mixture in the freezer and use electric beaters or a fork to give the ice cream a good stir and break up the ice crystals every 20 minutes or so. When the mixture is quite stiff, divide it among the moulds and freeze until hardened completely. Dip the moulds in hot water and turn out the kulfi. Sprinkle with the remaining pistachio kernels and decorate with edible silver leaf (varak), if you like.

Crème brûlée

This soft custard has a topping that's caramelized to a hard toffee crust.

Cooking time 1 hour
Serves 6

600 ml (21 fl oz) thick (double/heavy) cream
1 vanilla bean
6 egg yolks
100 g (3½ oz) caster (superfine) sugar, plus extra for topping

Put the cream in a saucepan. Split the vanilla bean in half, scrape out the seeds and add the bean and seeds to the saucepan. Heat slowly until almost boiling. Remove from the heat and set aside to infuse for 10 minutes. Remove the vanilla bean.

Whisk the egg yolks and sugar until thick and pale and then pour the cream onto the egg mixture, whisking constantly. Cover and set aside for 1 hour.

Preheat the oven to 140°C (275°F/Gas 1). Strain the mixture into six 150 ml (5 fl oz) ramekins and fill almost to the top. Put the ramekins into a baking tray and fill with enough hot water to come three-quarters of the way up the sides of the ramekins. Put in the centre of the preheated oven and cook for 30–40 minutes or until just set. Allow to cool, then cover and chill for at least 8 hours.

To serve, sprinkle each ramekin with an even layer of caster (superfine) sugar. Put the ramekins in a large baking dish and pack ice around the side to prevent the custards being heated. Put under a very hot preheated grill (broiler) and grill until the sugar caramelizes. The sugar must caramelize quickly so the custard doesn't have time to melt. If your grill does not get particularly hot you might want to invest in a mini blowtorch, which also does the job well. Serve within 1 hour of grilling.

Slow-baked quinces in honey

The origins of this dish can be traced to medieval France.

Cooking time 4 hours
Serves 8

60 g (2¼ oz) unsalted butter, softened
8 ripe quinces
60 g (2¼ oz) honey
125 ml (½ cup) sweet white dessert wine, such as Sauternes

Preheat the oven to 150°C (300°F/Gas 2). Use half the butter to grease a shallow, ceramic dish large enough to take the halved quinces in one slightly overlapping layer.

Peel and halve the quinces. Don't worry about them discolouring as they will turn very dark during cooking. Cut out and discard the cores. Put them cut-side-up in the prepared dish. Drizzle the honey on top and dot with the remaining butter. Pour the wine over the surface. Cover with foil and bake for 2 hours. Turn them over and return to the oven for another 2 hours. The quinces will turn a rich maroon red and the juices will caramelize. Serve hot with whipped cream or softened vanilla ice cream.

Roasted caramel pears

Pears with just a little caramel sweetener are elevated to the truly sublime.

Cooking time 4 hours
Serves 6

6 firm, ripe pears
1 lemon
460 g (2 cups) caster (superfine) sugar
1 cinnamon stick
2 tablespoons butter
splash of natural vanilla extract

Preheat the oven to 160°C (315°F/Gas 2–3). Peel the pears then cut them in half down their lengths, keeping the stems intact. Do not remove the core and seeds.

Put in a large bowl and squeeze over the juice of one lemon and toss to combine. Add enough cold water to cover the pears while you prepare the caramel — this will prevent them from browning. Put the sugar in a heavy-based saucepan with a cup of water and stir over a high heat until the sugar dissolves. Add the cinnamon stick and bring to the boil. Allow to boil, untouched, until the colour starts to take on a light golden hue. Watch your pot closely, carefully swirling the syrup around to evenly distribute the colour until you have a dark golden caramel with a sweet toffee scent — this will take about 8 minutes. Do not allow the caramel to burn. Remove the caramel from the heat and add the butter and vanilla, stirring until the butter melts.

Remove the pears from the water and put cut-side-down on a large baking tray. Pour over the caramel and put in the oven. The caramel will have set slightly but should start to melt again after it has been in the oven for a short while. As soon as it begins to melt, start to spoon it over the pears then continue to do so every 20–30 minutes for the next 3½–4 hours. The pears are ready when they are an even colour all the way through and have become quite transparent. Serve them warm, drizzled with caramel and juices. You can refrigerate the pears in their sauce for up to 4 days and reheat them in a warm oven.

Glossary and index

anise This herb is a member of the parsley family. The leaves and seeds have a sweet liquorice flavour and are used in both sweet and savoury dishes.

baking beads Small ceramic or metal beads which are used to weigh down a pastry case while the pastry is partially cooked, before being filled. Also known as pie weights.

besan (chickpea) flour Common in Indian cooking, besan flour is made from dried, ground chickpeas. Also known as gram flour, it can be stored in an airtight container in the refrigerator for up to 6 months.

black mustard seeds Substitute with brown mustard seeds if necessary.

blanch To cook in boiling water for a few minutes and then refresh in cold water. Blanching keeps the colour in vegetables and loosens tomato and fruit skins.

blind bake To bake a pastry case while it is unfilled in order to set the pastry. The pastry case is usually lined with baking paper or foil and filled with baking beads to stop the sides collapsing or the base from bubbling up.

Calvados A brandy from Calvados in the Normandy region of France, made with apples. It is often used in recipes for chicken, pork and veal.

celeriac A knobbly root vegetable. Choose a small, firm celeriac with as smooth a surface as you can find and store it in a plastic bag in the refrigerator for up to 7 days. When it has been peeled and cut, soak the pieces briefly in a bowl of water mixed with the juice of half a lemon to prevent discoloration.

chine To cut through the ribs of a joint close to the backbone so that the backbone can be removed to make carving easier. Ask your butcher to do this when you buy the joint.

clarified butter Useful because of its ability to withstand high cooking temperatures without burning. To make clarified butter, heat a packet of butter until it is liquid. Leave it to rest until the white solids settle to the bottom, then skim off any foam and strain off the golden liquid, leaving the solids behind. Let the liquid set and store it in the refrigerator.

clay pot Also known as a sand pot, this earthenware lidded pot is used for dishes that need to be cooked slowly on the stove. Clay pots can be fragile and should be heated slowly, preferably with a liquid inside.

Cognac A very fine French brandy, from Cognac in western France. It is double-distilled from wine and flavoured with caramel and sugar.

cornmeal Coarsely ground, dried wheat kernels, often used to make polenta or cornbread. It is available in varying grades for different purposes.

crème fraîche A thickened, lightly fermented cream, often used in place of regular cream in the French kitchen. It has a slightly tart taste.

crostini These small, thin slices of bread have been brushed with oil and then toasted until they are quite dry and hard. They are served with a savoury topping.

dang gui (dried angelica) A bitter Chinese herb, related to the European herb angelica. It can be found in Chinese grocery stores or herbalists and looks like small bleached pieces of wood.

dariole mould A small (individual-sized) castle-shaped mould.

deglaze To use a liquid to loosen the residue stuck to the bottom of a pan after frying. Stock, water or wine is added to the hot pan and the pan is scraped and stirred. The liquid is then added to the dish or used to make a flavoursome gravy.

ditalini Very small, short pasta tubes, often used in Italian soups.

dry-roast To toast spices in a pre-heated pan, without oil, to deepen and improve their flavour.

fermented red bean curd Cubes of bean curd steeped in a strong, fermented red sauce. Found in jars in Chinese grocery stores.

ghee Butter which has been melted and then simmered until all of the water has evaporated, giving it a nutty flavour. It has a very high smoking point and is available from some supermarkets or Indian grocers.

gratin dish A round or oval, shallow, ovenproof dish, which increases a dish's surface area, ensuring a larger portion of the crispy topping for each serving.

harissa A fiery red paste of North Africa, traditionally made of chilli peppers which are soaked, then pounded with coriander, caraway, garlic and salt, and moistened with olive oil.

horseradish, fresh Cultivated for its pungent, spicy root, horseradish is often used in condiments or sauces. Peel before use, but not too deeply — the greatest concentration of flavour is just under the skin.

Indian bay leaves (tejpat; thej patha; tajpattar) Used widely in Indian cooking, these are available from Indian grocers. Normal bay leaves are not a suitable substitute. Substitute one clove for each leaf if necessary.

jujubes Also known as Chinese dates or red dates, jujubes are an olive-sized dried fruit with a red, wrinkled skin. They need to be soaked before use.

juniper berries Blackish-purple berries with a resinous flavour and woodland aroma. They are used in stews and robust game dishes. Crush the berries lightly with the back of a knife before use to release their flavour.

Kashmiri chilli powder Made from dried Kashmiri chillies, and a very bright red in colour. Kashmiri chilli powder may be available at Asian grocery stores or can be replaced with a mild–medium chilli powder.

kefalotyri cheese A hard, salty Greek cheese, made from goat or sheep milk. Pecorino cheese may be used instead if you can't find it.

lasagne verde Sheets of pasta that have been coloured green by using English spinach in the dough.

makrut (kaffir) lime leaves Double-lobed leaves of the makrut (kaffir) lime tree. They have a tangy, citrus flavour and are popular in Asian cuisine. They are available fresh or dried and are increasingly likely to be found as 'makrut' lime leaves rather than sold as 'kaffir' lime leaves

Mandarin pancakes Often sold as Peking duck wrappers, these are available from some supermarkets or Asian grocery stores. Steamed bread may be used instead.

mandolin A handy machine used to cut fruits or vegetables to a uniform size or thickness. Make sure yours has a safety guard to protect fingers.

Mexican chocolate A bitter chocolate which is grainy in texture and quite different from the more common Swiss-style chocolate. In Mexico it is used to make hot chocolate and mole, a sauce that is often served with chicken.

muscovado sugar Also known as Barbados sugar, this is a raw, dark brown sugar which has a moist, fine texture.

pandoro Pandoro is the sweet, bread-like, traditional Christmas cake of Verona in Italy. Its golden colour results from the use of eggs and butter in the recipe. Traditionally star-shaped, it is soft and light, and contains no fruit.

passata Meaning 'puréed', this term most commonly refers to a smooth, uncooked tomato pulp bought in tins or jars. Best without added flavourings.

pie funnel These small, often ceramic, funnels sit in the middle of a pie, poking through the crust. They allow steam from the filling to vent, resulting in crisper pastry and fewer boil-overs.

pomegranate molasses A thick, tangy-sweet syrup, made by reducing pomegranate juice to the consistency of molasses. Also known as pomegranate syrup, it is available from speciality stores and Middle Eastern grocers.

powdered mace The dried and ground membrane of the nutmeg seed. It should be available from the spice section of your supermarket.

preserved mustard cabbage Also called Sichuan pickle or preserved vegetables, this is the root of the mustard cabbage preserved in chilli and salt. It is available whole and shredded in jars, plastic sachets or tins from Chinese shops.

rock sugar Yellow rock sugar comes as uneven lumps of sugar, which may need to be further crushed before use if the lumps are very big. It is a pure sugar that gives a clear syrup and makes sauces shiny and clear. You can use sugar lumps instead.

sesame oil, roasted Chinese sesame oil is made from roasted white sesame seeds and is a rich amber colour. Buy small bottles as the oil loses its aroma quickly. It does not fry well, but you can sprinkle it on food as a seasoning or use it mixed with another oil for stir-frying.

Sichuan peppercorns Not a true pepper, but the berries of a shrub called the prickly ash, Sichuan peppercorns have a pungent flavour and the aftertaste is numbing, rather than simply hot. They should be crushed and dry-roasted to bring out their full flavour. They are also known as Japanese pepper and are available from Asian grocers and some supermarkets.

snake beans Also called yard-long beans, these are about 40 cm (15 in) long. The darker green variety has a firmer texture.

soy sauce This sauce comes in two styles. Light soy sauce, which is also known as superior soy sauce or simply as soy sauce, is used with fish, poultry and vegetables. Dark soy sauce is more commonly used with meats. Buy small bottles and store in the fridge.

star anise An aromatic ingredient in Chinese cooking, this is a star-shaped dried seed pod containing a flat seed in each point. It has a flavour and aroma similar to fennel seed and aniseed.

Taleggio cheese A mountain cheese originally from the Italian Alps near Bergamo. Taleggio is a very good table and cooking cheese and should be eaten young. It is made in squares and has a pink-yellow crust and creamy centre.

Thai basil This has a lemony aroma and a more spicy flavour than normal basil. The leaves are elongated and a light shade of green. Available from Asian grocers.

water chestnuts The rhizomes of a plant that grows in paddy fields in China. The raw nuts need to be peeled with a knife and blanched, then stored in water. Tinned ones need to be drained and rinsed. Freshly peeled nuts are sometimes available from Chinese shops.

won ton wrappers Also called won ton skins, these are usually square and are made from wheat flour and egg. They are found in plastic sachets in the refrigerated cabinets in Chinese shops and good supermarkets, and can be frozen until needed.

yellow bean sauce This is actually brown in colour and is made from fermented yellow soya beans mixed with rice wine and dark brown sugar. There are various flavours and textures available (some types have whole beans in them). The sauce is sold under different names — crushed yellow beans, brown bean sauce, ground bean sauce and bean sauce.

A

Apple crumble 178
Asparagus risotto 22

B

Baccalà alla gratinata 134
Baked polenta with four cheeses 138
Baked Southern-style sticky ribs 104
Baked trout with fennel and capers 136
Beef and beet borsch 14
Beef carbonade 90
Beef cooked in ragù 88
Beef in Barolo 86
Boeuf bourguignon 94
Boeuf en croûte 92
Boeuf en daube 36
Bouillabaisse 18
Boulangère potatoes 163
Brandade de morue 70
Bread and butter pudding 172

C

Calamari ripieni 74
Cardamom chicken 60
Celeriac mash 163
Chicken with 40 cloves of garlic 119
Chicken, mushroom and tarragon
  pie 120
Chilli beef with capsicum, coriander
  and avocado 32
Chinese broccoli in oyster sauce 159
Chocolate and almond torte 166
Chocolate pots with hazelnut
  toffee 168
Coq au vin 56
Cottage pie 96
Coulibiac 132
Couscous 146
Crème brûlée 184
Crispy skin duck 68

D

Duck confit 66
Duckling with turnips 130

F

Florentine roast pork 102
French onion soup 13

G

Gigot d'agneau 112
Grilled polenta 144

H

Harira (chickpea, lamb and coriander
  soup) 13

I

Italian duck in red wine 124
Italian-style spicy sausage and bean
  casserole 41

K

Kulfi 184

L

Lamb braised with beans 44
Lamb shanks with tomato, chilli
  and honey 108
Lamb tagine 46
Lasagne al forno 98

M

Marmite dieppoise 76
Mashed potato 159
Mechoui 110
Milanese risotto 148
Minestrone alla Genovese 13
Moghul-style lamb 48
Moroccan chicken stew 58
Moussaka 114

N

Navarin of lamb 106
New York cheesecake 170

O

Octopus in red wine stew 72
Onion tart 26
Osso buco 50

P

Pear and almond tart 182
Pommes Anna 159
Pork noisettes with prunes 41
Pork with apples 100
Potato and leek al forno 163

Potato gnocchi 163
Poulet au pot 65
Poulet Vallée d'Auge 65
Prawn bisque 16

R

Rabbit fricassée 54
Red vegetable curry 78
Red-cooked pork 41
Risotto nero 20
Roast chicken 119
Roasted caramel pears 184
Rogan josh 42

S

Sautéed spinach 152
Slow-baked quinces in honey 184
Slow-cooked salted duck breasts 128
Slow-roasted balsamic tomatoes 159
Slow-roasted beef with beets and
  horseradish cream 84
Soy chicken 65
Spanish duck with smoked paprika,
  pears and toasted almonds 126
Spiced cabbage 154
Spicy roast chicken in banana
  leaves 119
Spinach koftas in yoghurt sauce 80
Sticky golden sponge pudding 174
Stifado 30
Stuffed guinea fowl 122
Stuffed vegetables Provençal style 140
Sweet paprika veal goulash 52

T

Tagliatelle with ragù 34
Tarte Tatin 180
Tian de legumes 150
Tres-leches (three-milk) cake 176

V

Vegetable terrine with herb sauce 24

W

Wet polenta 144
White bean purée 152

Soups

Beef and beet borsch	14
Bouillabaisse	18
French onion soup	13
Minestrone alla Genovese	13
Harira (chickpea, lamb and coriander soup)	13
Prawn bisque	16

Starters

Asparagus risotto	22
Onion tart	26
Risotto nero	20
Vegetable terrine with herb sauce	24

Beef

Boeuf bourguignon	94
Beef carbonade	90
Beef cooked in ragù	88
Boeuf en croûte	92
Boeuf en daube	36
Beef in Barolo	86
Chilli beef with capsicum, coriander and avocado	32
Slow-roasted beef with beets and horseradish cream	84
Stifado	30
Tagliatelle with ragù	34

Pork

Baked Southern-style sticky ribs	104
Florentine roast pork	102
Italian-style spicy sausage and bean casserole	41
Pork noisettes with prunes	41
Pork with apples	100
Red-cooked pork	41

Lamb

Gigot d'agneau	112
Lamb braised with beans	44
Lamb shanks with tomato, chilli and honey	108
Lamb tagine	46
Mechoui	110
Moghul-style lamb	48
Navarin of lamb	106
Rogan josh	42

Veal

Osso buco	50
Sweet paprika veal goulash	52

Rabbit

Rabbit fricassée	54

Chicken and poultry

Cardamom chicken	60
Chicken, mushroom and tarragon pie	120
Chicken with 40 cloves of garlic	119
Coq au vin	56
Moroccan chicken stew	58
Poulet au pot	65
Poulet Vallée d'Auge	65
Roast chicken	119
Soy chicken	65
Spicy roast chicken in banana leaves	119
Stuffed guinea fowl	122

Duck

Crispy skin duck	68
Duck confit	66
Duckling with turnips	130
Italian duck in red wine	124
Slow-cooked salted duck breasts	128
Spanish duck with smoked paprika, pears and toasted almonds	126

Seafood

Baked trout with fennel and capers	136
Brandade de morue	70
Calamari ripieni	74
Coulibiac	132
Marmite dieppoise	76
Octopus in red wine stew	72

Vegetarian

Baked polenta with four cheeses	138
Red vegetable curry	78
Spinach koftas in yoghurt sauce	80
Stuffed vegetables Provençal style	140

Mince

Baccalà alla gratinata	134
Cottage pie	96
Lasagne al forno	98
Moussaka	114

Accompaniments

Boulangère potatoes	163
Celeriac mash	163
Chinese broccoli in oyster sauce	159
Couscous	146
Grilled polenta	144
Mashed potato	159
Milanese risotto	148
Pommes Anna	159
Potato and leek al forno	163
Potato gnocchi	163
Sautéed spinach	152
Slow-roasted balsamic tomatoes	159
Spiced cabbage	154
Tian de legumes	150
Wet polenta	144
White bean purée	152

Desserts

Apple crumble	178
Bread and butter pudding	172
Chocolate and almond torte	166
Chocolate pots with hazelnut toffee	168
Crème brûlée	184
Kulfi	184
New York cheesecake	170
Pear and almond tart	182
Roasted caramel pears	184
Slow-baked quinces in honey	184
Sticky golden sponge pudding	174
Tarte Tatin	180
Tres-leches (three-milk) cake	176